# Depression in Childhood and Adolescence

# Depression in Childhood and Adolescence

## A Guide for Practitioners

Rebecca A. Schwartz-Mette
Hannah R. Lawrence
Douglas W. Nangle
Cynthia A. Erdley
Laura A. Andrews
Melissa S. Jankowski

**MP** **MOMENTUM PRESS**
HEALTH

First published in 2017 by
Momentum Press®, LLC
222 East 46th Street, New York, NY 10017
www.momentumpress.net

ISBN-13: 978-1-60650-935-7 (print)
ISBN-13: 978-1-60650-936-4 (e-book)

Momentum Press Child Clinical Psychology "Nuts and Bolts" Collection

Cover and interior design by S4Carlisle Publishing Services Private Ltd., Chennai, India

First edition: 2017

10 9 8 7 6 5 4 3 2 1

Printed in the United States of America

# Abstract

*Depression in Childhood and Adolescence: A Guide for Practitioners* fills a gap in the literature by providing practitioners with a "go to" resource for understanding, assessing, and treating youth depression. All in one source, practitioners will find easy-to-follow and clearly worded coverage of diagnosis, biopsychosocial conceptualization, assessment, and treatment, as well as special topics including gender and developmental differences, suicidality, and the use of antidepressant medication in treatment. Cutting-edge information is supplemented with illustrative case studies designed to bring key points to life. This volume is an excellent resource for practitioners and trainees across a variety of fields including child/adolescent psychology and psychiatry, developmental psychology, clinical social work, and school psychology.

# Keywords

Depression, Children, Adolescence, Diagnosis, Assessment, Conceptualization, Evidence-Based Treatment, Case Studies

# Contents

# Acknowledgments

The authors thank Dr. Samuel Gontkovsky and Momentum Press for their enthusiasm and energy in developing this important series of practitioner resources. The authors also acknowledge the researchers, study participants, therapists, and therapy clients that contributed to the development of their knowledge base regarding child and adolescent depression.

# CHAPTER 1

# Description and Diagnosis

*Luis is an 11-year-old student who, during a routine physical with his pediatrician, complains of headaches and stomachaches, especially on school days. His parents describe how Luis, once an avid baseball player, now spends weekends in bed playing video games. Teachers note that Luis appears touchy and isolates himself from his peers. When asked what he feels is the problem, Luis shrugs and says, "I don't know."*

Health care professionals regularly encounter youth like Luis, whose presentation could be typical of early adolescence or could signal something more serious. Children and adolescents commonly experience sadness, irritability, boredom, sleep and appetite changes, and school avoidance as they navigate the many challenges of development. Yet, for some, these symptoms occur at a level indicative of more severe emotional issues, such as the presence of a depressive disorder.

# What Is Depression?

Depression affects millions of children and adolescents each year (Center for Behavioral Health Statistics and Quality, 2015). A diagnosis of a depressive disorder represents a distinct set of clinical symptoms involving disturbances of mood, cognitions, and behavior. As will be discussed, depression leads to functional impairment across multiple domains (e.g., school, family, social; Nagar et al. 2010) and confers risk for continued emotional problems as youth enter adulthood (Pine et al. 1999; Weissman et al. 1999). As such, understanding how best to conceptualize, assess, and treat depression in childhood and adolescence is critical to preventing long-term distress.

Although decades of theory and research have been dedicated to understanding depression in adults, our knowledge about depression in children and adolescents has developed only recently. In fact, until about 25 years ago, many experts did not recognize that youth could experience depression at all (Weissman and Klerman 1992). Since the realization that youth could present with mood disorders, a wide body of research has attempted to clarify the experience of depression in childhood. This text synthesizes current research for practitioners and provides the "nuts-and-bolts" of diagnosing, conceptualizing, assessing, and treating depression in children and adolescents.

# Prevalence

Prevalence rates of clinical depression in children are quite low, at less than 1 to 2 percent (Birmaher et al. 1996; Costello et al. 2003). However, risk for depression increases sharply at adolescence (Hankin et al. 1998). Prevalence rates during adolescence can vary widely across studies (Roberts, Attkisson, and Rosenblatt 1998), but generally speaking, 7 to 8 percent of adolescents meet diagnostic criteria for a depressive disorder, a rate similar to that of depression in adults.

Risk for depression is especially pronounced for adolescent girls. Although girls are equally likely to experience depression as boys in childhood (Birmaher et al. 1996), by adolescence, the risk for depression increases dramatically for girls but remains stable for boys (Nolen-Hoeksema 2001). The greatest gender discrepancy occurs between ages 15 and 18 years (Hankin et al. 1998) with uneven gender ratios continuing into adulthood. Many factors contribute to girls' increased risk, including unique biological and social changes (Thapar et al. 2012; see Chapter 2 for an extended discussion of gender differences).

Despite the sizeable percentage of youth with identifiable depressive disorders, these prevalence estimates underestimate the scope of the problem. Depression goes underdiagnosed more frequently in youth than adults (Thapar et al. 2012), and less than 40 percent of youth diagnosed with mood disorders actually receive treatment (Merikangas et al. 2011). Additionally, many more youth do not meet diagnostic criteria for a depressive disorder, but nevertheless experience considerable distress and impairment related to subclinical depressive symptoms (Merikangas, Nakamura, and Kessler 2009). Estimates of the prevalence of subclinical depressive symptoms range from 5 to nearly 30 percent, depending on the study (Balazs et al. 2013; Wesselhoeft et al. 2013). Youth with subclinical symptoms are also at increased risk for later development of a depressive disorder (Thapar et al. 2012).

## Course and Chronicity

The course of depression tends to be episodic and chronic. On average, youth with depressive disorders are first diagnosed between 11 and 14 years of age (Dunn and Goodyer 2006; Merikangas, Nakamura and Kessler 2009), with girls experiencing earlier onset of first depressive episode than boys (Lewinsohn et al. 1994).

On average, episodes of depression last between 7 and 9 months (Birmaher et al. 1996). Approximately 60 to 90 percent of youth can be expected to recover within 1 year (Dunn and Goodyear 2006), but risk of recurrence is high. In fact, a majority of those who recover will experience additional depressive episodes within 5 years (Birmaher et al. 1996; Dunn and Goodyer 2006). Rates of recurrence tend to be higher for females than males and for those who have had multiple depressive episodes compared to those with only a single episode (Lewinsohn et al. 2000). Moreover, depression during childhood or adolescence is associated with an increased risk of depression during adulthood (Birmaher et al. 1996), as well as associated problems, such as anxiety disorders, substance-use disorders, bipolar disorder, suicidality, unemployment, and physical health problems (Thapar et al. 2012).

## Symptoms and Diagnosis

*The Diagnostic and Statistical Manual of Mental Disorders* (DSM-5; American Psychiatric Association 2013) is widely used to diagnose depressive disorders in childhood and adolescence. A DSM-5 diagnosis of major depressive disorder (MDD) requires that five (or more) of the following symptoms be present within the same two-week period:

- Depressed mood most of the day, nearly every day
- Markedly diminished interest or pleasure in all, or almost all, activities most of the day nearly every day
- Significant weight gain or weight loss when not dieting (e.g., change of more than 5 percent of body weight in 1 month), decreased or increased appetite nearly every day, or failure to make expected weight gains
- Insomnia or hypersomnia
- Psychomotor retardation or agitation
- Fatigue or loss of energy
- Feelings of worthlessness or excessive/inappropriate guilt
- Diminished ability to think or concentrate, or indecisiveness
- Recurrent thoughts of death, suicidal ideation, specific plan for suicide, or suicide attempt

Youth diagnosed with depression may manifest five (or more) of these symptoms; thus, not all depressed youth have the exact same symptoms. However, to be diagnosed using the DSM-5, one of the symptoms must be either depressed mood or diminished interest in activities. Symptoms must be present most of the day, nearly every day (as opposed to having an occasional "down day") and must cause clinically significant distress or impairment in social, academic, and other important contexts that represents a measurable change from previous levels of functioning. Importantly, these symptoms are endorsed through youth self-report or through the observations of others, such as parents, friends, teachers, and health care professionals. Finally, for a diagnosis of depression, the symptoms cannot be attributable to the physiological effects of a substance or other medical condition or be better explained by another disorder.

Though the diagnostic criteria for MDD do not necessarily differ for children and adolescents as compared to adults, the symptoms may present differently. For instance, youth may present with marked irritability as opposed to appearing only sad or tearful (Stringaris et al. 2013). Moreover, there is some research to indicate that children may report or display more physical or somatic symptoms of depression, whereas the cognitive symptoms (e.g., rumination) become more pronounced in adolescence (Bhatia and Bhatia 2007; Lakdawalla, Hankin, and Mermelstein 2007).

## Differential Diagnosis

Major depression is often difficult to distinguish from other, closely related conditions and disorders that also feature depressed mood as a prominent symptom. This section discusses multiple diagnoses that may also present with accompanying depressed mood in children and adolescents. Prior to discussion of differential diagnosis, however, it is important to acknowledge that periods of sadness in response to even minor hardships or daily hassles are a normal part of human living and especially common in adolescence. These periods of sadness should not be characterized as depression unless diagnostic criteria are met.

Intense sadness and other symptoms of depression may follow a loss, as in bereavement. Grief and depression indeed share many symptoms, including sadness, disturbed sleep, and change in appetite. Children and adolescents dealing with grief may also have thoughts of death related to their desire to be reunited with the person who died (Dowdney 2000). However, grief and depression are considered distinct constructs. This is not to say, however, that bereavement cannot precede a major depressive episode; in fact, loss often does trigger clinical depression (Lloyd 1980). An individual who experiences depressive symptoms following a loss could be diagnosed with MDD if and only if his or her symptoms meet full diagnostic criteria (American Psychiatric Association 2013).

In addition to developmentally normal periods of sadness and grief following loss, short periods of depressive symptoms may arise in response to a major stressor. Adjustment disorder with depressed mood is a short-lived episode of depressive symptoms that arises within 3 months of a stressor, but does not last longer than 6 months after the stressor has abated. Individuals with adjustment disorder are further distinguished from those with MDD in that they do not meet full diagnostic criteria for a depressive episode.

Persistent depressive disorder (dysthymia) is a longer-term, chronic condition that shares many symptoms with MDD. Youth with dysthymia experience depressed mood nearly every day (which may present as irritable mood in youth) for at least 1 year. They also must have two or more of the following: increased/decreased appetite, insomnia/hypersomnia, low energy or fatigue, low self-esteem, concentration problems, and feelings of hopelessness. Importantly, during the one-year period, the youth must not have been without these symptoms for more than 2 months at a time, whereas depressive episodes as a part of MDD are episodic in nature (i.e., symptoms remit at some point in time). Additionally, MDD includes additional possible symptoms that are absent in persistent depressive disorder (e.g., anhedonia, psychomotor retardation/agitation, suicidality). It is also important to consider that the prevalence of dysthymia is typically lower than that of MDD (Merikangas, Nakamura and Kessler 2009).

In recent decades, increasing attention has been paid to bipolar I and II disorders, as well as cyclothymia, in childhood and adolescence. Bipolar disorders are far less common in youth than MDD (Angold and Costello 2001). However, it can be difficult to initially determine whether a youth is suffering from unipolar depression (e.g., MDD) or a bipolar mood disorder, as both include periods of depression (e.g., depressive episode). However, unlike MDD, bipolar disorders involve episodes of abnormally and persistently elated, expansive, or irritable mood during which other manic symptoms (e.g., grandiosity, significantly decreased need for sleep, pressured speech, flights of ideas, distractibility, heightened energy and engagement in goal-directed activities, excessive involvement in risky behavior) also are present. Cyclothymia represents a subclinical form of bipolar disorder in which neither full criteria are met for hypomanic episode nor depressive episode, yet multiple subclinical hypomanic and depressive episodes are present across a period of at least 1 year.

Finally, depression also can be induced by substance use (substance-induced mood disorder) and certain medical conditions (mood disorder due to another medical condition).

---

### Depression or Bipolar?

Clinicians can struggle to differentiate depression from bipolar disorder in youth, as many symptoms associated with these syndromes can overlap, be a part of normal development, or both.

When considering a diagnosis of bipolar I or II disorder, remember that youth with bipolar disorders tend to have circumscribed periods of grandiose, elated, or irritable mood accompanied by (hypo)manic symptoms such as:

- Significantly decreased need for sleep w/o fatigue
- Pressured speech
- Engagement in risky behavior

and separate periods of depressed mood or anhedonia accompanied by:

- feelings of worthlessness/guilt
- changes in sleep/appetite
- fatigue.

Remember that youth with bipolar disorders also can have mixed episodes (i.e., periods of both depressive and (hypo)manic symptoms). For more information, see the Bipolar Disorder Resource Center at www.aacap.org.

---

## Associated Conditions

Unfortunately, depression in childhood and adolescence places youth at heightened risk for the development of many associated problematic conditions (i.e., comorbidity; Costello et al., 2003). Between 40 and 70 percent of depressed youth have one comorbid condition and 20 to

50 percent have two or more comorbid conditions (Birmaher et al. 1996). Rates of comorbidity are especially high in adolescents with more severe depression (Thapar et al. 2012). Having two or more disorders also predicts more severe impairment, poorer longer-term outcomes, and poorer response to treatment (Thapar et al. 2012).

The most frequent condition to co-occur with depression is anxiety. Adolescents with depression are 6 to 12 times more likely to have clinical levels of anxiety (Costello, Foley, and Angold 2006), such as generalized anxiety, social or specific phobia, obsessive-compulsive disorder, or separation anxiety disorder (Birmaher et al. 1996; Costello et al. 2003). Interestingly, it is unclear whether anxiety leads to depression or vice versa, as research finds that anxiety predicts later depression and that depression also predicts later anxiety (Costello et al. 2003).

Compared to youth without depression, depressed youth also are at significantly increased risk for externalizing issues, such as problems with attention, conduct, and substance use. Children and adolescents with attention-deficit/hyperactivity disorder (ADHD) are often diagnosed with depression, potentially because of shared genetic predispositions underlying both conditions, or because depression may occur as a result of dealing with ADHD (Wilens, Biederman, and Spencer 2002). Regarding conduct problems, adolescents with depression are 4 to 11 times more likely to have a disruptive behavior disorder than adolescents who are not depressed (Costello et al. 2006). Additionally, 20 to 30 percent of youth with depression have a substance-use disorder as well (Birmaher et al. 1996).

Along with experiencing increased risk for comorbid conditions, youth with depression suffer dysfunction in multiple contexts (see Chapter 2 for extended discussion). In addition to the cognitive impairments associated with depression itself (e.g., indecisiveness, difficulty concentrating), depression in youth is associated with other cognitive problems, such as negative beliefs about self and others, internal attributions for personal failures, and external locus of control (McCauley, Mitchell, Burke, and Moss 1988). Youth with depression also tend to experience academic impairments, such as poor attendance, low grades and levels of achievement, and greater dissatisfaction with school (Roeser, Eccles, and Strobel 1998). Social impairments, such as rejection and withdrawal, are also common for youth with depression. Finally, depression is associated with a variety of health-risk behaviors, such as high-risk sexual behavior, non-suicidal self-injury, and suicidality.

Given the prevalence of depressive disorders in youth, clinicians are likely to frequently encounter this syndrome and its associated challenges. The following chapters will address conceptualizations of the etiology and maintenance of depression (Chapter 2), the assessment of depression (Chapter 3), and treatment of depression (Chapter 4). Chapter 5 includes two case vignettes to illustrate concepts covered in Chapters 1 to 4.

# CHAPTER 2

# Conceptualization

## At a Glance

- What Causes Depression?
- Behavioral Conceptualizations
- Cognitive Conceptualizations
- Interpersonal Conceptualizations
- Biological Conceptualizations
- Integrative Theory: The ABC Model of Depression

## What Causes Depression?

Multiple theories exist to explain the development of depression in youth. Behavioral, cognitive, interpersonal, and biological perspectives on child and adolescent depression have flourished in recent decades. The contemporary theoretical focus has shifted toward integrating these perspectives into comprehensive models that acknowledge the multifaceted nature of depression. Integrated theories have contributed greatly to our understanding of the multiple pathways that may lead to depression, particularly for populations at heightened risk, such as adolescent girls. Following a review of behavioral, cognitive, interpersonal, and biological theories, (see Figure 1), this chapter focuses on one such integrated model, the Affective, Biological, Cognitive (ABC) Model of Depression (Hyde, Mezulis, and Abramson 2008), in conceptualizing the development of depression in youth. Specific vulnerabilities related to gender and development are highlighted throughout.

## Behavioral Conceptualizations

Behavioral theories focus on learning principles to explain the development of depression. Specifically, behavioral theories posit that depression arises from difficulties interacting with the environment such that an individual's positive behaviors are not adequately rewarded. As such, these positive behaviors occur less frequently and eventually cease through extinction (i.e., a lack of response contingent positive reinforcement; Lewinsohn 1974). Following the removal of positive reinforcers, the individual begins to interpret his/her behavior as meaningless and to feel a lack of control, contributing to learned helplessness, negative affect, and, eventually, depression. For example, a depressed youth may withdraw from activities that he/she previously enjoyed, such as athletics. As a result, the youth does not experience the positive reinforcement he/she once did (e.g., sense of physical well-being, praise from coaches, social interaction with teammates). This lack of positive reinforcement may then lead to feeling more depressed.

Negative experiences within the context of relationships (and resulting reinforcement and/or punishment) are conceptualized as falling within the domain of behavioral conceptualizations of depression. In this chapter, the implications of negative family and general peer experiences will be discussed in terms of behavioral approaches, whereas more nuanced interpersonal processes will be discussed in the context of interpersonal theories.

# Parent–Child Model of Socialization

Within behavioral theories of depression, the Parent–Child Model of Socialization (Pomerantz 2001) has been applied in understanding the development of depressive symptoms. This model contends that when parents frequently use intrusive support, children who hold negative self-evaluations are more vulnerable to depressive symptoms than children who have positive self-evaluations. Pomerantz (2001) found evidence that both parents and children may contribute to the development of depressive symptoms.

Within the family context, interparental conflict and divorce have been identified as important variables to consider. Greater exposure to frequent, intense, and poorly resolved interparental conflict is associated with an increased risk for internalizing problems (Rhoades 2008). Children and adolescents who experience their parents' divorce also may be at elevated risk for depression, especially during the period of kindergarten to 5th grade compared to the 6th to 10th grades (Lansford et al. 2006). These age differences may be because of issues such as young children being less capable of understanding the causes of divorce, feeling more anxious about abandonment, or being more isolated from outside social support.

In addition to the family, youths' peer relationships play a critical role in their adjustment (Parker and Asher 1987). Peer rejection and victimization, friendship problems, and romantic relationship functioning all have been implicated in the development of depression. Children who are rejected by their peers have higher levels of depressive symptoms than those who are not rejected (e.g., Boivin, Poulin, and Vitaro 1994). Similarly, numerous studies have found a strong association between peer victimization experiences (e.g., aggression, exclusion) and depression (see Hawker and Boulton 2000 for a meta-analysis). Relational forms of victimization (involving attacking one's reputation or sense of belonging) are more strongly related to depression than are overt (physical) forms of victimization (La Greca and Harrison 2005; Prinstein, Boergers, and Vernberg 2001), particularly during adolescence (La Greca and Harrison 2005) and for girls (Prinstein, Boergers, and Vernberg 2001). Evidence further suggests that the relation between victimization and depression is reciprocal, where initial victimization predicts depression, which predicts increased victimization over time (Hodges and Perry 1999).

Another important aspect of peer experience is friendship, defined as a close, mutual, dyadic relationship (Hartup 1996). Friendships tend to be characterized by companionship, intimacy, and validation, although friendships can differ in quality. Many studies demonstrate that the stressful experience of not having a friend or of being involved in a low-quality friendship is associated with higher depressive symptoms in children and adolescents (e.g., La Greca and Harrison 2005; Preddy and Fite 2012). Having fewer friends (e.g., Kingery, Erdley, and Marshall 2011) and having poor quality friendships (e.g., Kamper and Ostrov 2013) predict increases in depressive symptoms over time. Depressive symptoms also predict declines in the number (for girls only, Rudolph, Ladd, and Dinella 2007), stability (e.g., Prinstein et al. 2005), and quality of friendships (e.g., Oppenheimer and Hankin 2011). Finally, regarding romantic relationships, La Greca and Harrison (2005) found that negative qualities of romantic relationships predicted depressive symptoms even when other peer relations and best friend qualities were considered. Thus, the stressful experience of having a low-quality romantic relationship may uniquely contribute to the prediction of adolescents' depressive symptoms.

As discussed, behavioral conceptualizations of depression and associated research suggest that a lack of positive reinforcement (or the presence of punishment) from the environment increases risk for depression in youth. One particularly relevant context for youth is social relationships, including family, peer, and romantic relationships. When relationships are problematic, youth may experience a lack of positive reinforcement and/or punishment from others, increasing risk for depression. See Interpersonal Conceptualizations section (below) for additional discussion of relationship interactions that may contribute to depressive symptomology.

### Cognitive Conceptualizations

Cognitive theories arose, in part, as a response to perceptions that behavioral theories failed to account for the role of thought processes (cognitions) in the development of depression. Cognitive theory holds that individuals' emotions and behaviors are influenced by the way they think (Beck 2011). Most cognitive models of depression are diathesis-stress models in which depression is thought to result from an interaction of cognitive vulnerability and environmental stress (Abela and Hankin 2008). Individuals with cognitive vulnerabilities have biased, negative, and self-focused information processing styles. This way of thinking about stressful events is believed to create a downward spiral into depression. Specific depression-related cognitive vulnerability factors have been identified in research with children and adolescents.

*Distorted thoughts and negative core beliefs.*    Distorted thoughts are negative, automatic appraisals of a situation (Beck 2011). For example, in response to a frustrating event, an individual may think, "Nothing ever works out for me." Distorted thinking may trigger cycles of biased information processing involving overgeneralization and catastrophizing. Over time, this may develop into what Beck called the "negative cognitive triad," which involves relatively stable, maladaptive views of the self, the world, and the future (e.g., Kaslow, Stark, Printz, Livingston, and Tsai 1992), otherwise known as core beliefs. Depression is thought to result when negative core beliefs become well established. During adolescence, girls demonstrate higher levels of negative thinking (e.g., Abela, Aydin, and Auerbach 2007) than boys.

*Depressogenic attributional style.*    Individuals with a depressogenic attributional style (Abramson, Seligman, and Teasdale 1978; Abramson, Metalsky, and Alloy 1989) tend to make attributions of negative events that are global (e.g., "Everyone hates me"), stable (e.g., "It's never going to change"), and internal (e.g., "It's all my fault"). Following negative life events, a depressogenic attributional style is associated with increased depressive symptoms for both children (Brozina and Abela 2006) and adolescents (e.g., Prinstein and Aikins 2004). In a recent study (Braet et al. 2015), negative views of the self and the future (but not the world) were also associated with depressive symptoms in children, whereas negative views of the self, world, and future were associated with depressive symptoms in adolescents. Braet et al. speculated that adolescents are able to engage in more abstract thinking than children, and are thus able to more effectively entertain a view of the world that impacts their emotional adjustment (2015).

*Rumination.*    The way youth respond to their depressed mood also has been implicated in the risk for developing depression. Specifically, a tendency to ruminate, or excessively think about one's own distress, its causes, and its consequences, in response to sad or low mood is thought to create a vulnerability for depression (Nolen-Hoeksema, 1991). Rumination predicts greater severity of depressive symptoms over time in children (e.g., Abela,

Brozina, and Haigh 2002) and adolescents (e.g., Abela and Hankin 2008; Michl et al. 2013), especially for girls (Abela et al. 2012; Hankin 2009).

*Low levels of self-perceived competence and low self-esteem.*    Low perceived competence and self-esteem are thought to be another vulnerability (e.g., Cole 1990; Cole 1991). Negative self-perceptions may develop in response to negative feedback from parents, teachers, and peers (e.g., Garber and Flynn 2001; Seligman et al. 1995). Indeed, research finds that low self-perceived competence and low self-esteem are both associated with increases in depressive symptoms for children (e.g., Cole et al, 2001; Sowislo and Orth 2013) and adolescents (Hoffman et al. 2000; Sowislo and Orth 2013; Van Tuijl et al. 2014). Further, Verboom and colleagues (2014) found that perceived social competence and depressive symptoms were bidirectionally related over time for both boys and girls, with stronger associations for girls.

*Self-criticism.*    Youth who are highly self-critical or overly concerned with interpersonal issues (i.e., sociotropy) may be prone to depression in the face of stressful events. Little and Garber (2005) found that high sociotropy was associated with negative interpersonal events, which in turn predicted increases in sixth-graders' depressive symptoms. Self-criticism may be an especially injurious vulnerability factor implicated in the development of depression for adolescents following negative achievement-related events (e.g., Abela, Sakellaropoulo, and Taxel 2007) and in the context of interpersonal stress (Auerbach, Ho, and Kim 2014).

Early views suggested that cognitive vulnerability to depression did not emerge until the transition from middle childhood to early adolescence. It was thought that younger children were not cognitively vulnerable to depression because of limitations in cognitive processing and the ability to think abstractly. Some studies were consistent with this view (e.g., Turner and Cole 1994). However, subsequent research that investigated a wider range of cognitive vulnerability factors (e.g., rumination, distorted thinking, self-criticism) has not revealed developmental differences (e.g., Abela, Aydin, and Auerbach 2007). Nevertheless, Abela and Hankin (2008) assert that it is likely that a great deal of change occurs in cognitive vulnerability across childhood and adolescence. They suggest that cognitive styles become more stable with development and may generalize such that youth acquire multiple cognitive vulnerabilities, partially explaining the increased risk for depression from childhood through adolescence.

Importantly, decades of research converge to demonstrate that the associations among cognitive vulnerabilities, stress, and depression are likely reciprocal. That is, although cognitive vulnerabilities and stress do predict depressive symptoms as noted above, depressive symptoms and cognitive vulnerabilities also predict future stress (Calvete, Orue, and Hankin 2013). Moreover, depressive symptoms and stress predict additional cognitive vulnerabilities (Calvete et al. 2013; Hamilton et al. 2015; Quiggle et al. 1992). As such, the relations of cognition, stress, and depressive symptoms are perhaps best understood as transactional.

### Interpersonal Conceptualizations

Interpersonal models of depression have emerged in recent years with increasing specificity regarding the interpersonal context of child and adolescent depression. Such models can be understood through the lens of behavioral theory (see above), but are separated for the purposes of deeper discussion here. Coyne proposed his initial interpersonal theory of depression (1976a) following observations of depressed adults (1976b). The theory holds that depressed individuals interact with others in ways that are aversive and that incite both guilt and hostility. As a result, depressed individuals erode their social supports as partners eventually reject them. Rejection increases the depressed individual's feelings of worthlessness, thereby exacerbating depression, and the cycle continues. Coyne also posited that partners who remain in relationships with depressed individuals are at risk for developing depression themselves, a process referred to as depression contagion (Coyne 1976a). Recent research has extended these theories to childhood and adolescence (e.g., Hammen 1991; Joiner and Barnett 1994; Prinstein et al. 2005). Studies have identified aversive interpersonal behaviors characteristic of depressed youth that contribute to relationship problems, which then may lead to increased depressive symptoms.

*Excessive reassurance seeking.* Excessive reassurance seeking (Joiner et al. 1999), defined as repeated requests for assurance that one is truly liked and/or cared for (Timmons and Joiner 2008), has received the most attention in the literature. The theory is that because depressed individuals have negative views of themselves (e.g., "I'm not okay") and others (e.g., "People don't like me"), they request reassurance from relationship partners in an effort to feel better. Unfortunately, however, the behavior is thought to be perceived as off-putting by others and may lead to rejection. In a sample of adolescents, Prinstein and colleagues (2005) found that excessive reassurance seeking predicted decreases in positive friendship quality as well as subsequent increases in depressive symptoms for girls.

*Negative feedback seeking.*    Negative feedback seeking is another potentially maladaptive interpersonal behavior involving depressed individuals seeking negative feedback that confirms (and may unfortunately exacerbate) their negative self-views (Timmons and Joiner 2008). Although studied nearly exclusively in adults (e.g., Swann et al. 1992), initial research with adolescents suggests that negative feedback seeking is associated with depressive symptoms and lower levels of peer acceptance (for boys, Borelli and Prinstein 2006).

*Conversational self-focus.*    Conversational self-focus, or the tendency to redirect conversations to focus on the self, may have similar consequences for depressed youth. In the context of adolescent friendships, conversational self-focus has been shown to be associated with depressive symptoms and lower positive friendship quality (Schwartz-Mette and Rose 2009) and to predict increased rejection by friends over time (Schwartz-Mette and Rose 2016).

*Co-Rumination.*    Not all depression-related interpersonal behaviors appear to be problematic for relationships. In fact, recent research has illuminated one behavior that has positive implications for relationships but negative consequences for emotional adjustment. Co-rumination is a dyadic behavior defined as excessively discussing problems with a focus on rehashing and speculating about problems and emphasizing negative affect (Rose 2002). Co-rumination is related to internalizing symptoms both concurrently (e.g., Calmes and Roberts 2008; Rose 2002) and over time (Rose, Carlson, and Waller 2007; Starr and Davila 2009), and even predicts onset of clinical depression (Stone et al 2011). Ironically, co-rumination is also associated with having high-quality friendships

(Rose 2002; Rose et al. 2007), likely because of the support and closeness friends feel when they share their distress with one another.

Co-rumination may be particularly salient for adolescent girls. Co-rumination is more common among girls than boys in both childhood and adolescence (Schwartz-Mette and Rose 2012). These gender differences are more pronounced in adolescents than in children, which is significant given that gender differences in friendship and emotional adjustment increase with age (Buhrmester and Furman 1987; McDougall and Hymel 2007). Although co-rumination is associated with positive friendship quality for both genders, it appears to exacerbate depressive symptoms only for girls (Rose et al. 2007; Stone et al. 2011).

*Depression contagion.*   Another interpersonal process relevant to the development of depressive symptoms is depression contagion, a well-documented phenomenon in which having a friend or relationship partner with depressive symptoms increases one's risk for developing depressive symptoms (Joiner 1994). Initial research documented the effect in adults (e.g., Joiner, Alfano, and Metalsky 1992), but more recent work has demonstrated that contagion effects are observed within same-sex friendships of adolescents (Giletta et al. 2011; Prinstein 2007; Stevens and Prinstein 2005) and children (Schwartz-Mette and Rose 2012) as well. Some evidence suggests that females may be more susceptible to contagion than males (Giletta et al. 2011). In line with this idea, co-rumination is one mechanism that facilitates depression contagion within adolescent friendships (Schwartz-Mette and Rose 2012; Schwartz-Mette and Smith in press).

### Biological Conceptualizations

Biological theories of child and adolescent depression focus on both genetic and neurobiological factors. Evidence strongly suggests that depression "runs in families" (Hammen 1991). That is, youth with a relative with depression are at greater risk for developing depression themselves. This finding has been established in family history, twin, and adoption studies (for a review, see Rice, Harold, and Thapar 2002). The familiality of depression is thought to result predominately from genetic influences (Sullivan, Neale, and Kendler 2000).

Though research on specific genes implicated in depression is still in its early stages, some studies have isolated particular gene variants that, in combination with life stress, are associated with enhanced depression risk. For example, in combination with child maltreatment, having the short allele (as opposed to long) version of 5-HTTLPR (i.e., the serotonin transporter-linked polymorphic region of the 5-HTT gene) has been implicated in increased risk for depression (Caspi et al. 2003). Additionally, following findings that the met allele on the Val66Met polymorphism of the brain-derived neurotrophic factor (BDNF) modulates the effect of adversity on adult depression (Aguilera et al. 2009), La Greca and colleagues (2013) found that stress is more strongly related to elevated depressive symptoms for youth with the met allele. Such literature may help begin to make sense of the fact that not all children who experience stress go on to develop depression (Rutter 2006; Rutter, Moffitt and Caspi 2006).

Weiss and colleagues (2006) have suggested that many genes including BDNF may behave differently in males and females. For example, estrogen is thought to affect levels of BDNF (Sohrabji and Lewis 2006). Additionally, Shalev and colleagues (2009) found evidence that a significant polymorphism in the BDNF gene modulates hypothalamic–pituitary–adrenal axis reactivity and regulation differently for men and women when experiencing stress. This preliminary work may be an important lead in future examination of gender differences in risk for depression.

## The Role of Stress

Although both boys and girls begin to encounter more stressors by age 13 years, this increase is especially pronounced in girls (Rudolph and Hammen 1999). This may explain, in part, the emergence of sex differences in depression during adolescence. Using a multiwave prospective design with 6th to 10th grade students, Hankin (2009) found that both a negative cognitive style and stressors explained why girls showed increasing trajectories of depressive symptoms over time as compared to boys. Similarly, a recent longitudinal study (Hamilton et al. 2015) revealed that adolescent girls also experienced higher levels of interpersonal dependent stress, and this explained girls' greater levels of rumination, which in turn accounted for higher levels of depressive symptoms in girls than boys.

Hormones also are thought to play a role in the development of depression, particularly with respect to onset of puberty. Secretion of DHEA (dehydroepiandrosterone, a hormone produced by the adrenal glands) precedes the pubertal process in humans. Research has speculated that the ratio of cortisol ("the stress hormone") to DHEA may be higher in individuals with depression and that elevated cortisol/DHEA ratios reflect persistence of depression in adolescence (Goodyer et al. 2001a; Goodyer et al. 2001b). Testosterone levels, which increase during puberty, have further been implicated in depression. Research with males with hypogonadism (a condition involving decreased testosterone) suggests that lower levels of testosterone may be associated with significantly higher levels of depressive disorder in males (Shores and Matsumoto 2014; Zarrouf et al. 2009). Interestingly, other research suggests that higher levels of testosterone may also negatively impact mood and contribute to the onset of depression in females (Rohr 2002).

Atypical (early or late) puberty may be related to onset of depression. Early puberty appears to be especially problematic for girls (Stice et al. 2001), whereas early or late puberty is associated with depression in boys (e.g., Kaltiala-Heino, Kosunen, and Rimpela 2003). Ge and colleagues (1996) suggest that girls who enter puberty early may not yet be psychologically prepared for the new stressors, different environments, and changing expectations that adolescence involves. Graber et al. (1997) found that boys entering puberty late had less social competence, greater depressive symptomology, and more school-related problems than on-time-maturing peers. Another study, however, demonstrated that early puberty predicted increases in depressive symptoms but only for boys and girls who were unpopular (Teunissen et al. 2011).

Finally, normative developmental brain changes also render adolescents and females particularly vulnerable to depression. During adolescence, the brain experiences additional synaptic pruning (resulting in more efficient and focused processing), rapid brain development (resulting in greater plasticity; Poletti 2009), and changes in the limbic system (resulting in reduced experience of positive reinforcement and lower levels of positive affect; Giedd 2008). These changes may contribute to adolescents' greater tendency to ruminate and more frequent experiences of decreased positive affect. As a result of cycling hormones in females, the adolescent female brain becomes sexually dimorphic from the male brain, leading to heightened stress responsiveness, which may partially account for emerging gender differences associated with risk for depression (Cameron 2004). Interestingly, differences in brain growth and volume have been observed between depressed and nondepressed adolescents. For example, depressed adolescents have been observed to have less growth in the hippocampus and less reduction in putamen volume (Whittle et al. 2014). Additionally, Vulser and colleagues (2015) found that adolescents with depressive symptomology were more likely to have reduced gray and white matter brain volumes in some regions, and that medial-prefrontal gray matter volume may be associated with depression, particularly for girls.

## Integrative Theory: The ABC Model of Depression

No one existing theory can explain the entirety of depression, but each theory offers important contributions about the multiple pathways to depression. Scholars have recently highlighted the need for integration from multiple theoretical frameworks to better understand depression. The ABC Model of Depression (Hyde et al. 2008) is an example, combining affective, biological, and cognitive risk factors into a vulnerability-stress model. These vulnerabilities emerge or intensify in early adolescence and tend to be stronger for girls.

In terms of affective factors, the ABC Model incorporates vulnerabilities such as temperament and negative emotionality. Genetic vulnerability, pubertal hormones, and pubertal timing are among biological components that are proposed to explain depression onset and gender differences. The ABC Model also incorporates negative cognitive style, rumination, and body image as specific cognitive vulnerabilities. Finally, the model accounts for the finding that girls experience greater life stress than boys, both with regard to broadly construed stress as well as specific stressors (e.g., sexual abuse, pressure to conform to gender roles). The ABC Model proposes that, beginning in adolescence, such negative life events interact with affective, biological, and cognitive vulnerability factors to explain girls' enhanced risk of depression.

As an example, an adolescent girl may be bullied by peers as a result of early puberty. She begins to ruminate about her appearance and seeks repeated reassurance from her boyfriend to confirm that she is attractive. Frustrated, her boyfriend breaks up with her, which leads to negative emotionality and decreased self-esteem. While none of the factors discussed above may directly lead to the development of depression, the combination of affective, biological, and cognitive factors could place her at an increased risk for developing depression.

## Conclusion

As discussed in this chapter, depression is a complex disorder that likely does not result from either genetic or environmental influences alone but rather from the interaction of both in the context of both gender and development. Current approaches to understanding factors that contribute to depression indeed reflect this integration and adopt an interdisciplinary approach to understanding depression. Such theories are well poised to inform approaches to assessment and treatment, which are discussed in Chapters 3 and 4, respectively.

# CHAPTER 3

# Assessment

## At a Glance

- Current Assessment Practices
- Types of Assessment
- Purposes of Assessment
- Issues in Assessing Children and Adolescents

Accurate assessment of children and adolescents with depression is critical to effective treatment. Assessment involves the integration of information from multiple measures and multiple informants throughout treatment. Indeed, the best assessment is comprehensive and ongoing, including assessment for the purposes of choosing a diagnosis, determining symptom severity, tracking treatment progress and outcomes, and understanding general functional impairment.

Assessment, like treatment, should be guided by empirical evidence. Increasing emphasis has been placed on evidence-based practice, which includes evidence-based assessment (EBA). Although EBA has received substantially less attention compared to evidence-based treatment, interest in empirically evaluating clinical assessment approaches has grown (Klein, Dougherty, and Olino 2005). EBA involves using empirical research to select psychometrically sound measures and methods appropriate for a specific assessment purpose, and to carry out the assessment process in an empirically guided manner (Hunsley and Mash 2010). Understandably, practitioners may find it especially difficult to conduct EBA when assessing youth, given the many available measures, need to consider the developmental level of the child or adolescent, and importance of gathering data from multiple sources (e.g., caregivers, teachers). Assessment with youth differs from that with adults in that multiple informants are used and the fact that youth self-report is often less reliable and valid (Chrisman et al. 2006). Another complicating factor is that depression may present differently by developmental stage (Dougherty et al. 2008). This chapter aims to provide clear, useful information regarding assessment of child and adolescent depression for multiple purposes and at different stages of treatment.

## Current Assessment Practices

Assessment has long been among the unique and defining features of the profession of psychology (Mash and Hunsley 2005). That being said, the majority of clinicians do not use standardized or empirically supported assessment measures. Instead, clinical child and adolescent psychologists report using clinical interviews most frequently (Cashel 2002). This is troubling, as unstructured clinical interviewing is prone to confirmatory biases in which clinicians fail to consider diagnoses outside of their initial impressions and tend to be less comprehensive than other assessment approaches. Given that use of assessment has repeatedly been shown to improve upon clinical decision making and to result in superior therapeutic outcomes compared to use of clinical judgment alone (e.g., Dawes, Faust, and Meehl 1989), the following section provides useful types of assessments to consider when evaluating child and adolescent depression (see Table 3.1 for brief overview of assessment options).

## Types of Assessment

### Diagnostic Interviews

Diagnostic interviews help clinicians determine whether a client's reported symptoms meet Diagnostic and Statistical Manual of Mental Disorders (or International Classification of Diseases) criteria for particular disorders. Interviews may be employed to assess depression as well as other forms of psychopathology, streamlining the processes of differential diagnosis and detection of comorbidity. It should be noted that children younger than 8 to 9 years old may not be capable of reporting valid information in diagnostic interviews (Angold and Fisher 1999). As such, parents and caregivers may be used as informants.

Interviews can be structured, semistructured, or unstructured. Structured interviews involve a clinician reading a set of prescribed questions and recording client responses. This approach does not allow for further questioning and/or interpretation. These interviews were developed with the intention of being used by lay interviewers, as less training and clinical expertise is needed to administer them (Orvaschel 2004).

Semistructured interviews are considered the gold standard of diagnostic assessment (Dougherty et al. 2008). They provide flexibility and incorporate clinical judgment while also ensuring that clinicians ask about critical symptoms and explore alternate diagnoses and comorbidity. Clinicians are guided by a framework (i.e., a set of questions) that directs information gathering with the flexibility to elicit further information from the client (Durbin and Wilson 2009). Thus, administration requires clinician training and experience. The Kiddie Schedule for Affective Disorders and Schizophrenia—Present and Lifetime version (K-SADS-PL; Kaufman et al. 1997) is recommended for use with youth and may be a particularly viable option for clinicians, given that it is free and has excellent psychometric properties.

Unstructured interviews involve clinicians guiding the interview of the client based on the clinician's judgment. The format of unstructured interviews varies widely in terms of duration, focus, and coverage, and they may, on average, be less comprehensive than structured or semistructured interviews (Angold and Fisher 1999; Durbin and Wilson 2009). Although unstructured interviews are a ubiquitous and important part of clinical practice, they alone are not typically recommended for diagnostic assessment with youth. Alternately, combining unstructured and (semi) structured approaches may be advantageous.

Currently, there is no diagnostic interview just for depression (for either children or adolescents). As previously mentioned, the *K-SADS-PL* is a good option for assessing a range of disorders including depression and is sensitive to treatment change. It is the most widely used semistructured interview for youth and is appropriate for clients aged 6 to 18 years. Depending on the severity of symptomatology, the average time to administer ranges from 35 minutes to 2.5 hours for parents and children. The K-SADS-PL must be administered by a trained clinician.

Other options include the *Diagnostic Interview Schedule for Children* (DISC-IV; Shaffer et al. 2000), a structured interview for youth aged 9 to 17 years and parents of 6- to 17-year-olds. It takes between 1 and 2 hours to administer and assesses multiple types of psychopathology. Because the DISC-IV is highly structured, it may be administered by clinicians with little training. Additionally, the *Child and Adolescent Psychiatric Assessment* (CAPA; Angold and Costello 2000), a semistructured interview for youth aged 9 to 17 years, may be used. Like the DISC-IV, administration time is 1 to 2 hours and the CAPA assesses a range of psychopathology. However, the CAPA also includes assessment of functional impairment across familial, peer, school, and social domains as well as an interviewer-based observational component of the child's behavior.

### Rating Scales

Depression rating scales include lists of depression symptoms. Respondents rate the degree to which each particular symptom applies to themselves or to the youth (if answered by a parent or guardian). In this category are questionnaires specifically designed to assess depressed mood as well as measures of overall functioning that include scales to assess depressive symptoms. Rating scales are useful for screening, establishing symptom severity, determining baseline level of functioning, and tracking progress over time (Orvaschel 2004). Additional advantages include that they are typically low cost and time efficient and that they may be able to provide information on phenomena that may not be readily observable by others (such as feelings of guilt/worthlessness, thoughts of suicide). Used in isolation, however, rating scales are not comprehensive enough to be used as a primary diagnostic tool (Durbin and Wilson 2009). Thus, it is recommended that they be used in conjunction with some type of diagnostic interview.

As of 2006, there were 280 measures of depressive symptom severity and this number is only growing (Santor, Gregus, and Welch 2006). A full review of available assessment instruments is beyond the scope of this chapter. Rather, this chapter highlights psychometrically sound and highly used assessment instruments for use with children and adolescents. The *Children's Depression Inventory* (now in its section edition, CDI 2;

Kovacs 2010) is the most frequently used self-report measure of youth depressive symptoms. For use with youth aged 7 to 17 years, the CDI 2 is brief (10 to 20 minutes to complete) with 28 items. The CDI 2 assesses key symptoms of depression and provides scales measuring emotional problems and functional problems and subscales that measure negative mood/physical symptoms, negative self-esteem, interpersonal problems, and ineffectiveness. The *Reynolds Child Depression Scale-2nd edition* (RCDS-2; Reynolds 2002) and *Reynolds Adolescent Depression Scale-2nd edition* (RADS-2; Reynolds 2004) also are popular scales assessing affective, cognitive, and physiological features of depression. The RCDS-2 is for children aged 7 to 13 years and the RADS-2 is for adolescents aged 11 to 20 years. Both scales include 30 items and take approximately 10 minutes to complete.

The *Children's Depression Rating Scale-Revised* (CDRS-R; Poznanski, Freeman, and Mokros 1985) is a clinician-administered rating scale for children aged 6 to 12 years based on a semistructured interview and behavioral observations. It is administered to youth and a caregiver, and the clinician uses judgment to combine the two reports. It takes 15 to 20 minutes to administer and assesses 17 symptom areas (e.g., depressed feelings, irritability suicidal ideation, social withdrawal, appetite disturbance, impaired school work). Finally, the *Center for Epidemiologic Studies of Depression-Revised* (CESD-R; Eaton et al. 2004) is a self-report scale including 20 items that mirror diagnostic criteria for major depression. It takes approximately 5 to 10 minutes to complete and is suitable for use with adolescents aged 13 to 18, and is free (Prinstein, Boergers, and Spirito 2001).

## Purposes of Assessment

### Screening

The purpose of screening is to identify youth who may be at a higher risk for depression and who may benefit from additional, more focused assessment. Given that depressive symptoms are relatively common, Birmaher and Brent (2007) recommend screening all children and adolescents for primary depressive symptoms (e.g., sad mood, irritability, anhedonia). Screening is particularly beneficial when a full, comprehensive assessment with every client is impractical. Many screening devices assess for

Table 3.1 Evidence-based assessments for youth

| Purpose | Instrument | Phase of assessment | | | | | Age range | Time to administer | Training required |
|---|---|---|---|---|---|---|---|---|---|
| | | Screening | Diagnostic | Symptom severity | Treatment progress and outcomes | Self-harm/ Suicide risk | | | |
| Diagnostic interviews | Schedule for Affective Disorders and Schizophrenia for School-Age Children—Present and Lifetime (K-SADS-PL) | | X | | | X | 6–18 | 35 minutes– 2.5 hours | Substantial |
| | Diagnostic Interview Schedule for Children (DISC-IV) | | X | | | X | Youth 9–17 and parents of 6–17 | 1–2 hours | Minimal |
| | Child and Adolescent Psychiatric Assessment (CAPA) | | X | | | X | 9–18 | 1–2 hours | Substantial |
| Rating scales | Children's Depression Inventory 2 (CDI 2) | X | | X | X | X | 7–17 | 15–20 minutes | None |
| | Reynolds Child/Adolescent Depression Scales (RCDS-2, RADS-2) | X | | X | | X | RCDS-2: 7–13 RADS-2: 11–20 | 10 minutes | None |
| | Children's Depression Rating Scale-Revised (CDRS-R) | X | | X | X | X | 6–12 | 15–20 minutes per informant | Minimal |
| | Center for Epidemiologic Studies Depression Scale-Revised (CESD-R) | X | | X | | X | 13–18 | 5–10 minutes | None |

multiple disorders, allowing clinicians to identify what type of follow-up assessment may be warranted (Durbin and Wilson 2009).

Ideally, screening measures are brief, low-cost, and easy to administer (Durbin and Wilson 2009). Typically, screening instruments consist of rating scales that can be either clinician-administered or completed by youth, parents, and/or teachers. Even the best rating scales, however, may have high rates of false positives and false negatives when it comes to actual clinical diagnosis (e.g., Kendall, Cantwell, and Kazdin 1989). As such, rating scales may have greater clinical utility as screening tools as opposed to diagnostic tools. Researchers have recommended the RCDS-2 and RADS-2 to be used in school and/or community samples and the CDRS-R and CDI 2 to be used in clinical samples (Dougherty et al. 2008).

## Diagnostic Assessment

The purpose of diagnostic assessment is to determine whether a client meets diagnostic criteria for a disorder and to rule out diagnoses that are also characterized by depressive symptoms (see Chapter 1 for specific diagnostic criteria). Recall that symptoms must be present most of the day, nearly every day and must cause clinically significant distress or impairment. Although diagnostic criteria do not differ between children and adolescents for MDD, the distinction between normality and abnormality may in part depend on the child/adolescent's developmental level (Durbin and Wilson 2009). For example, anxiety, somatic symptoms, temper tantrums, and noncompliance are more characteristic of depression in early childhood; cognitive symptoms, dysphoric mood, self-esteem issues, and hopelessness are more characteristic of depression in middle and late childhood; and sleep and appetite problems, suicidal ideation and attempts, and overall impairment of functioning are more characteristic of depression in adolescence (Birmaher, Brent, and Benson 1998).

Also important to consider when diagnosing youth, the reliability and validity of youth self-reports are less consistent than for adults. Thus, information must be obtained from additional informants (e.g., parents, teachers; Chrisman et al. 2006). Diagnosis using multiple informants results in greater reliability and validity of diagnosis than diagnoses based on a single informant (Thapar et al. 2012). The child or adolescent may provide the best report of internal symptoms or subjective states while a caregiver/teacher can add to the description of observable or external symptoms. While research indicates that discrepancies can exist between symptoms reported by youth (especially younger children) and symptoms reported by parents and teachers (e.g., Achenbach, McConaughy, and Howell, 1987), it is recommended that reports of all parties be considered together.

Clinical interviews and rating scales are the primary means of diagnostic assessment (Dougherty et al. 2008). Semistructured interviews are considered the gold standard of diagnostic assessment. Caution should be used when using rating scales in isolation to obtain a diagnosis, as they typically focus on current symptoms (i.e., do not also ask about duration of symptoms and exclusion criteria) and are often confined to a specific domain (e.g., depressive symptoms only), precluding adequate differential diagnosis and/or assessment of comorbidity.

### Assessing Symptom Severity

Symptom severity is key to determining baseline functioning, informing treatment choice, and identifying treatment targets. Depressive symptom severity occurs along a continuum (e.g., Widiger and Clark 2000), and varying degrees of severity may influence treatment. For instance, greater severity of depressive symptoms is associated with poorer treatment response (e.g., Goodyer et al. 1997). Additionally, youth with subthreshold depression (i.e., high levels of symptoms that do not meet diagnostic criteria for a depressive disorder) experience distress and impairment, placing them at risk for future psychopathology. As such, they may warrant treatment or follow-up assessment. Assessing for initial severity also helps to determine whether medication may be useful in treatment (Dougherty et al. 2008) and what treatment setting may be most appropriate (e.g., inpatient vs. outpatient). For example, inpatient treatment may be indicated if a youth's suicidality is not well managed in an outpatient setting.

Rating scales (completed by youth and caregivers) are primarily used to assess symptom severity. They are low cost and quick to administer, so that assessment can potentially be administered to multiple informants and repeatedly administered across treatment.

## Assessing Treatment Progress and Outcomes

Assessing treatment progress involves repeatedly measuring change in symptoms and/or impairment to determine whether treatment should continue, be altered, or be discontinued (Dougherty et al. 2008). Knowing whether clients are improving helps clinicians enhance outcomes for clients (Lambert, Hansen, and Finch 2001). In general, parents appear to be less sensitive to change in youth's depressive symptoms than youth themselves (Dougherty et al. 2008). As such, it is important to obtain reports from both youth and their caregivers. Clinicians also may wish to evaluate symptoms and impairment at termination. Surprisingly, only 8 percent of child and adolescent psychologists reported routinely assessing treatment outcome (Cashel 2002). What is more, when treatment outcomes are assessed, most clinicians use clinical observation and judgment rather than objective measures (Garland, Kruse, and Aarons 2003). Assessing outcomes is not only important for clinicians to evaluate treatment, but it also provides the client with a meaningful index of change, which may increase self-efficacy.

## Assessing Associated Problems

A comprehensive assessment not only measures depression symptoms, but also family, social, and academic functioning and related concerns (Durbin and Wilson 2009). A well-rounded assessment enhances case conceptualization and treatment planning. One aspect of interest to clinicians is the degree to which depressive symptoms are impacting daily life. Depression is known to impact functioning across multiple domains, including school, home, and peer contexts (Dougherty et al. 2008). Assessing functioning across these domains provides clues as to why depression may have developed, uncovers possible maintaining factors that can serve as additional treatment targets, and identifies factors that may impede treatment gains (Dougherty et al. 2008; Durbin and Wilson 2009). Such broad assessment likely requires use of a multimethod, multi-informant approach (Durbin and Wilson 2009).

Assessing for stressful life events may also be important to clinicians. Stressors (e.g., loss, conflict, rejection) predict onset of depression (Goodyer et al. 2001a), and chronic stress may also maintain depressive episodes (Dougherty et al. 2008). Unfortunately, depression can elicit and/or result in additional stressors (e.g., peer conflict). Semistructured interviews are best suited to assess for the presence of stressors, establish the temporal relationships between stressor and onset of depression, and determine whether stressors currently maintain the depression. For adolescents, it may be beneficial to assess for interpersonal stress, given that social stress is especially salient during the adolescent developmental period.

Family history of depression is also important to consider in the development and maintenance of youth depression. Parental depression is associated with poorer treatment outcomes for children (e.g., Brent et al. 1998). If there is a family history of depression, it may be beneficial to recommend parental treatment and also may warrant further assessment of how family interactions may be maintaining depression in both youth and their parents.

Comorbidity is the rule, not the exception, in depression, as two-thirds of depressed adolescents have at least one comorbid condition and 10 to 15 percent experience two or more (Thapar et al. 2012). Compared to nondepressed adolescents, depressed adolescents have 6 to 12 times risk for anxiety, 4 to 11 times risk for a disruptive behavior disorder, and 3 to 6 times risk for substance use, with comorbidity rates even higher for youth with more severe depression (Costello et al. 2006; Thapar et al. 2012). As comorbidity predicts poorer response to treatment (Durbin and Wilson 2009), it is important to assess comorbidity to determine primary treatment targets, whether other disorders need to be monitored/treated, and whether additional diagnoses may hamper treatment progress (Dougherty et al. 2008). Diagnostic interviews are often not disorder specific and thus can provide a structured or semistructured framework for assessing not only depression, but possible comorbidities as well.

### Assessing Suicide Risk

Rates of youth suicide have increased over the previous three decades (Curtin, Warner, and Hedegaard 2016) and continue to rise. Given that depression is a leading risk factor for suicide for children and adolescents (Dougherty et al. 2008; Gould et al. 1998), assessment of depression should also include assessment of suicidality. Suicidality includes thoughts about suicide (ideation), suicide planning, suicide gestures and rehearsals, suicide attempts, and death by suicide. It is recommended that all youth be asked not only generally about suicide, but also specifically about current ideation, specific plans, previous and recent attempts, and availability of means to enact a suicide plan (Orvaschel 2004). Comprehensive assessment of risk for suicide allows clinicians to take appropriate steps to fully ensure client safety. Many measures used to assess depressive symptom severity in youth include an item or items addressing suicidality (e.g., CDI 2 item 8; CESD-R items 14 and 15; CDRS-R item 13; RADS-2 item 14). Particular attention should be paid to these critical items to determine whether follow-up questions or possible intervention is needed.

A common misperception about risk assessment is that inquiring about suicide somehow increases suicidality or 'gives' a client suicidal ideas. Indeed, clinicians and caregivers alike worry that asking about suicide will trigger suicidal thoughts and/or actions (Feldman et al. 2007). However, asking nonsuicidal individuals about suicide does not appear to enhance risk for suicide (e.g., Lawrence and Ureda 1990). For individuals who experience some suicidality, asking about suicide allows for possible intervention (e.g., Murphy 1975). Moreover, in a study with adolescents, no harmful effects of asking about suicide were found (Gould et al. 2005).

## Issues in Assessing Children and Adolescents

Assessing depression in children and adolescents presents unique challenges. As noted, there are limitations to relying on youths' self-reports of symptoms, especially in younger children whose linguistic, cognitive, and emotional recognition abilities are more limited (Durbin and Wilson 2009). Younger children also tend to minimize socially undesirable symptoms (Cantwell et al. 1997), have difficulties reporting symptom duration and onset (Durbin and Wilson 2009), and provide unreliable accounts of temporal information (e.g., Chrisman et al. 2006). Thus, parents should be involved in assessment (Dougherty et al. 2008).

Disagreement between informants also is a perennial issue. Youth and their caregivers typically do not agree on assessments of depressive symptoms (Jensen et al. 1999), with children reporting less depressive symptomology than parents or clinicians (Kendall et al. 1989). Discrepancies only increase through adolescence (Durbin and Wilson 2009), potentially because of parents being more highly involved in the day-to-day lives of children compared to adolescents (Dougherty et al. 2008).

Low inter-rater agreement does not imply that some raters must be wrong or inaccurate. Members of a youth's system, including the youth him/herself, may have discrepant beliefs about what is normal behavior, and youth also may exhibit different symptoms in different settings (Cantwell et al. 1997). Importantly, youth, caregiver, and teacher reports are all found to be valid predictors of psychopathology in youth (Jensen et al. 1999).

Methods exist for addressing disagreement between informants. Durbin and Wilson (2009) discuss the "or" and "and" approaches. The "or" approach counts a symptom as present if any informant reports it, whereas the "and" approach counts a symptom as present only if it is reported by multiple informants (Durbin and Wilson 2009). Research suggests that the "best estimate" approach to making diagnoses is often highly reliable (Klein et al. 1994). This approach uses clinician judgment to take all assessment information into account to determine whether the youth meets criteria for a depressive disorder (Klein et al. 2005). In practice, a clinician typically follows this approach and uses clinical judgment to integrate information from multiple informants to come to the most accurate diagnostic decision (Durbin and Wilson 2009). The clinical practice of assessment would greatly benefit from additional research on how best to integrate information gathered from multiple informants.

## Conclusion

Clinicians' use of EBA with youth may significantly enhance outcomes for depressed youth. In terms of best practices, it is suggested that when diagnosing depression, clinicians utilize semistructured diagnostic interviews, which provide structure while allowing for use of clinical judgment. Use of multiple informants including the child (if over 8 to 9 years) or adolescent as well as a caregiver(s) provides various important perspectives on the problem. It is recommended that clinicians use the "best estimate" approach when disagreement between informants is observed.

It is also critical to assess the potential for associated problems, including comorbidity, functional impairment, life stressors, and suicidality. Finally, ongoing monitoring of treatment progress (using child and caregiver reports) is key in order to check the effectiveness of the intervention and to adjust accordingly where appropriate.

# CHAPTER 4

# Treatment

## At a Glance

- Current Practices
- What Works in Psychotherapy?
- Evidence-Based Approaches
  - CBT
  - IPT
- Psychotropic Medication
  - Medication Plus CBT
  - Suicide Risk
  - Conclusions
- Putting it All Together

The treatment of child and adolescent depressive disorders is complex. The development of depressive disorders is multifaceted and includes high rates of negative reinforcement, low rates of positive reinforcement, negative cognitions, precipitating stressful events, predisposing vulnerability factors, and a lack of protective factors (e.g., social skills). Fortunately, the multiple factors implicated in the etiology of depression illuminate many targets for intervention (Clarke and DeBar 2010). This chapter reviews current evidence-based practices for treating youth depression, including cognitive-behavioral and interpersonal approaches.

# Current Practices

The best snapshot of current outpatient practices comes from a review by Olfson and colleagues (2003). Reviewing health care expenditures from 1996 to 1999, the authors examined youth between the ages of 6 and 18 years who were treated for depression. Each year only 1 percent of youth received outpatient treatment for depression, a number well below the estimated prevalence rates of 2 to 8 percent. Thus, at best, only about half of the diagnosed youth get treated. Of those youth who were treated, 79 percent received psychotherapy, 56.9 percent medication, and 47.1 percent a combination of the two. On average, they attended 7.8 sessions per year, although a third had only one to two visits. A majority (76.7 percent) were seen by physicians, with smaller percentages seen by psychologists (33.8 percent), social workers (6.3 percent), or more than one provider (29.3 percent).

Though comprehensive and focused squarely on depression, the Olfson et al. (2003) study is somewhat dated. More recent investigations of general outpatient practices suggest that the proportion of youth being treated exclusively with medication has increased (Olfson and Marcus 2010; Olfson et al. 2013). The provider picture has also changed and primary care physicians are playing a much more prominent role in treatment (Mark, Levit and Buck 2009).

With regard to typical psychotherapy treatment, Weersing and Weisz (2002) provide insight. They conducted a study comparing treatment-as-usual (TAU; i.e., community mental health, most often psychodynamic approaches) to that provided in the context of randomized clinical research trials (RCTs) of cognitive-behavioral therapy (CBT) for youth aged 7 to 17 years diagnosed with depression. To maximize generalizability, youth with comorbid disorders were allowed in the study, and 52 percent of the sample identified as a racial or ethnic minority. Youth in the RCT conditions experienced more rapid and longer-lasting relief as compared to those receiving TAU, and this effect was not attributable to initial depression levels or to comorbidity. Minority youth and those receiving a low dose of treatment had worse outcomes, although when comparing minority and low-dose participants across treatments, those receiving CBT fared better. TAU was comparable to control conditions in the RCTs, indicating no evidence for the effectiveness of TAU (see also Weiss et al. 1999).

# What Works in Psychotherapy?

The summary above paints a rather bleak picture. We know that too few youth get treatment of any kind, and, of those treated, many get some form of psychotherapy that may or may not be evidence-based or effective. There is, however, a silver lining. Effective, evidence-based psychotherapy treatments do exist. This section briefly summarizes what the research tells us about what specific forms of psychotherapy work with depressed youth.

Reflecting a broader movement toward evidence-based practice in medicine, clinical psychology began the process of identifying a list of "empirically supported treatments" in the mid-1990s (Chambless and Hollon 1998; Task Force on Promotion and Dissemination of Psychological Procedures 1995). Over the years, this effort evolved into the identification of "evidence-based treatments" in recognition of the fact that treatment selection should involve a consideration of the research evidence, clinical expertise, and client characteristics (APA Presidential Task Force on Evidence-Based Practice 2006).

Key to this process was the establishment of criteria for evidence-based treatments (Chambless et al. 1998; Chambless and Hollon 1998; Chambless et al. 1996; Lonigan, Elbert, and Bennett 1998). *Well-established* treatments are those with at least two well-conducted, between-group design experiments demonstrating that the treatment is better than medication, placebo, or other treatment, or that it is equivalent to an already established treatment. Treatment must be guided by a manual, sample characteristics must be detailed, and studies must be conducted by at least two independent research teams. *Probably efficacious* treatments are those with at least two experiments demonstrating that the treatment is more effective than a no-treatment control group (e.g., waitlist) or that the studies meet all of the criteria for well-established status except the requirement that the studies are conducted by two different groups.

In 2008, David-Ferdon and Kaslow published an authoritative review of the existing evidence-based treatment studies for depressed youth. Therapies from two major theoretical orientations met the criteria for the top two tiers: CBT and interpersonal psychotherapy (IPT). Specific results are somewhat complicated to interpret because CBT has many different formats. For example, it is delivered in both individual and group formats, with and without parents, and although a broad approach (e.g., CBT) may meet the criteria for one tier, a specific exemplar [e.g., self-control therapy, Coping with Depression-Adolescents (CWD-A)] may not. For example, CWD-A contributes to the well-established status of CBT, but has not been evaluated by an independent research group. More specific descriptions of CBT and IPT approaches are found below.

In their review, David-Ferdon and Kaslow (2008) discuss the difference between efficacy and effectiveness trials. Efficacy studies are tightly controlled experimental evaluations usually conducted in laboratories or university settings. These studies are important because they can show that a given treatment is responsible for improvements, as opposed to chance or other factors. Effectiveness studies, in contrast, evaluate the treatment in "real-world" conditions (e.g., clinic-referred cases with co-morbidity) and are important for generalizability of efficacy research. Most research evidence is based on efficacy trials, which is problematic because youth treated in efficacy trials may not resemble youth in typical treatment settings. For example, most efficacy study participants are fairly homogeneous, with less severity and comorbidity than that is typically present in clinical practice. Similarly, there is under-representation of diverse patient characteristics, such as ethnicity and race, in many research trials (Weersing and Weisz 2002). Efficacy studies for depressed youth are also typically conducted in school settings, rather than a clinic, rendering the generalizability of efficacy studies, at this time, somewhat questionable.

## Evidence-Based Psychosocial Treatments for Depression

Psychosocial treatments are most effective for mild and moderate depression. As noted, the most widely studied and empirically supported psychosocial treatments are CBT and IPT. In CBT, maladaptive thought and behavior patterns linked with depressed mood are identified and new skills are learned to alter such patterns, thus improving mood. In doing so, CBT aims to improve coping, emotion regulation, problem-solving, and social skills (Stark et al. 2006). In IPT, an area of interpersonal difficulty linked with the client's depressed mood is identified and skills are

## The Evidence For CBT: Children

*Well-established* CBT programs for depression involve group therapy. Programs for children (Stark, Reynolds, and Kaslow 1987) are typically carried out in school settings and include psychoeducation, self-monitoring of pleasant events, cognitive restructuring, problem solving, and social skills training. Group approaches for children involving parents also are well-established (e.g., Stark, Rouse, and Livingston 1991). Similar to children-only groups, parent-involved group therapy for children involves parent and family meetings to support new skill acquisition and to support increases in pleasant events. *Probably efficacious* CBT programs include self-control therapy for children (Stark, Reynolds, and Kaslow 1987), a group-based intervention involving psychoeducation, self-monitoring of pleasant events, and problem solving focused on improving social behavior.

Although individual CBT for children has not yet reached either well-established or probably efficacious status, adaptations of group CBT for individual children (e.g., in private practice settings) is an informed approach that is likely to be more effective than adopting non-evidence based approaches.

established to navigate the issue effectively, reducing depression symptoms and improving interpersonal functioning. While CBT and IPT differ in theoretical orientation, they share several common treatment components. Both involve psychoeducation and can target change in both distorted cognitions and dysfunctional interpersonal relationships (Stark et al. 2006). The components of CBT and IPT, as well as examples of each, are discussed below.

### Cognitive-Behavioral Therapy

Within the cognitive-behavioral model, multiple forms of youth CBT exist, all of which involve core strategies of psychoeducation, behavioral activation, and cognitive restructuring. Aside from these central features, different CBT manuals contain different combinations of additional treatment components including strategies that aim to improve youths' coping, emotion regulation, and problem-solving and social skills. Manuals also differ in format of treatment delivery such as the amount of structure/flexibility, individual versus group formats, and the sequence of treatment (Jeffreys and Weersing 2014). Research has identified common treatment components (Chorpita and Daleiden 2009; Kaslow et al. 2014), discussed below.

*Psychoeducation.*   One of the first steps in CBT is psychoeducation, informing the youth about the nature of depression and its treatment. Psychoeducation may include teaching the cognitive-behavioral model of depression and how negative distorted thoughts, behavior common to depression (e.g., disengagement in previously enjoyed activities), and depressed mood interact to maintain depression. Skill deficits (i.e., emotion regulation or problem-solving skills) that may underlie depression are reviewed, and the family's role in depression may also be discussed (Stark et al. 2006).

---

## The Evidence for CBT: Adolescents

Adolescent groups (e.g., Lewinsohn et al. 1990) involve basic cognitive-behavioral techniques but focus additionally on communication and conflict resolution. As with children, there are no *well-established* individual CBT treatments for adolescent depression. Adolescent group therapy (Lewinsohn et al. 1990) involves separate parent groups that reinforce the content taught in the adolescent group sessions.

Individual CBT (with or without parents) for adolescents also is *probably efficacious* (Brent et al. 1997). The content is similar to the group approaches, just in an individual therapy format.

---

*Behavioral activation.*   Behavioral activation encourages more frequent engagement in a variety of pleasurable activities. Youth create a list of activities they would like to do more often and then track how often they participate in such activities, as well as their mood. This allows youth to recognize the relationship between doing enjoyable activities and improvements in how they feel (Clarke and DeBar 2010). Participation in activities reduces social withdrawal and provides opportunities for positive reinforcement, and may be a way to experientially challenge distorted thoughts (Stark et al. 2011).

*Cognitive restructuring.*    Another key component of CBT is identifying distorted, negative thoughts. Maladaptive thoughts can be identified using a thought record where youth record the thoughts they experience when feeling down or depressed. These thoughts are then challenged by examining evidence that the thought is true or false, identifying errors in thinking, evaluating the effects of thinking this way, and considering alternative viewpoints. Negative thoughts are then replaced with more positive and realistic thoughts (Clarke, Lewinsohn, and Hops 1990). Over time, cognitive restructuring is believed to change the child's underlying negative schemas (Stark et al. 2006).

*Affective education and mood monitoring.*    Youth are taught to recognize symptoms of depression and to notice changes in their emotions. As they become more sensitive to changes in their symptoms throughout treatment, mood monitoring alerts them to implement their coping, emotion regulation and problem-solving skills (Stark et al. 2011). Mood monitoring involves youth tracking symptoms of depression and mood over time to monitor progress and provide evidence of improvement. This evidence serves to reinforce the child's improvements.

*Problem solving.*    Problem solving is taught to help youth change situations that are within their control and are distressing or undesirable. Problem-solving strategies may include identifying the problem, generating possible solutions to the problem, evaluating each solution (e.g., pros and cons), and implementing the best decision.

*Coping strategies.*    Youth with depression typically have deficits in coping skills. Adaptive coping skills (e.g., relaxation, emotion regulation) are introduced and practiced for use in instances where a problem or undesirable situation is out of the youth's control. Regular use of effective coping can improve depressive symptoms, as youth learn to notice positive changes in mood and attribute these positive changes to specific coping strategies (Stark et al. 2006).

*Parent education/training.* Some CBT programs include a parent group or optional parent component. Parents can serve as a support system, provide insight into their child's functioning, and may also benefit from involvement in treatment as parent behavior may serve to maintain child depression (Chung and Fristad 2014). Positive parenting and effective discipline are taught to ameliorate misbehavior that can co-occur with depression. Since depression can strain parent–child relationships, some programs also have parents develop communication skills to encourage parental empathy for the child. Family problem-solving or conflict resolution skills may also be taught to reduce conflict within the home (Stark et al. 2011).

### Illustrative CBT Examples

Although many CBT protocols exist, the ACTION program (Stark et al. 2007) and the CWD-A (Clarke et al. 1990) incorporate many of the treatment components discussed above. Both are considered well-established group treatments for children and adolescents, respectively, and can be adapted for individual therapy.

*ACTION.* The ACTION program (Stark et al. 2007) is a highly structured, school-administered group treatment for girls 9 to 13 years of age consisting of 20 group sessions and 2 individual sessions. A parent training component helps parents listen empathically, model problem-solving and cognitive restructuring skills, structure a supportive home environment, improve family communication, and reinforce children's positive behaviors (Stark et al. 2010).

The program aims for children to learn and apply coping skills to manage depressive symptoms, recognize problems that are in their control and apply problem solving, recognize negative thoughts, and apply cognitive restructuring to build positive core beliefs (Stark et al. 2010). Girls learn and practice skills through in-session activities and are later encouraged to apply the skills to real-life problems in guided homework assignments (Stark et al. 2006).

The first half of treatment focuses on psychoeducation, affective monitoring, and learning coping and problem-solving skills through group activities and homework. Girls learn about depression and the CBT model, including how treatment will help them manage their depression. Emotional self-awareness is taught by encouraging youth to become "emotion detectives" by investigating the experience of their Body, Brain, and Behavior (the three Bs). Youth are also taught to cope with negative emotions when situations are out of their control, for instance, doing something fun or relaxing or seeking social support (Stark et al. 2010). Step-by-step problem solving is taught in a developmentally appropriate manner as the "5 Ps": problem identification and definition (Problem), goal identification and definition (Purpose), solution generation (Plan), consequential thinking (Predict and Pick), and self-evaluation (Pat on the back).

The second portion of treatment focuses on practicing coping and problem-solving skills, cognitive restructuring, and developing a positive sense of self. Five categories of coping skills include doing something fun and distracting, doing something soothing and relaxing, doing something that expends energy, talking to someone, and changing thoughts. Youth are also taught to recognize negative and distorted thoughts about themselves, their experiences, and their future. Girls are also encouraged to be "thought judges" to determine the validity of their negative thoughts by asking two questions: (1) What is another way to think about it? (2) What is the evidence? (Stark et al. 2006). When youth have difficulty letting go of negative thinking, it is referred to as "getting stuck in the negative muck." Youth are encouraged to utilize cognitive restructuring strategies to talk back to their negative thoughts (i.e., "the Muck Monster").

*Adolescent coping with depression course.*   The CWD-A (Clarke et al. 1990) is a highly structured mixed-gender group intervention for 13- to 18-year-olds across 14 two-hour sessions in 7 weeks. CWD-A is grounded in a model that proposes that there are multiple pathways to depression, but that learning cognitive and behavioral skills can improve coping strategies to overcome depression (Clarke and DeBar 2010). Homework is an especially important aspect of this treatment, as it provides adolescents with opportunities to practice and generalize new skills.

Treatment includes skills training modules, each targeting a specific symptom or skill deficit (Clarke and DeBar 2010). The behavioral activation module increases engagement in pleasant activities to improve interpersonal interactions and reduce social withdrawal. The cognitive restructuring module targets feelings of guilt and worthlessness by identifying, challenging, and replacing distorted, negative thoughts with more realistic, positive beliefs. The relaxation training module teaches progressive muscle relaxation and deep breathing techniques to reduce social anxiety that may inhibit participation in pleasant events. A social skills module teaches adolescents how to appropriately initiate and maintain relationships. The communication training module corrects negative social behaviors by practicing listening, providing feedback, and effective interpersonal problem solving. Of note is that the CWD-A program also involves parents to practice conflict negotiation and problem-solving skills. Near the end of the program, adolescents establish short- and long-term goals, identify potential barriers, and generate solutions regarding how best to attain these goals (Clarke and DeBar 2010).

*Example of individual treatment.*   Clarke and colleagues (2005) developed a brief, individualized adaption of CWD-A, allowing for flexible customization of treatment to individual adolescents. This shorter, collaborative-care CBT program takes place over five to nine individual sessions. The program includes two modules: cognitive restructuring and behavioral activation. The youth and therapist determine which module to begin first based on previous therapy and preferred coping strategies. The length of treatment is based on the child's response to the first half of treatment (Clarke and DeBar 2010). This program is often provided in conjunction with medication, so the therapist also addresses medication compliance and communicates the benefits and side effects of the medication to the youth's prescribing health care provider.

### IPT for Depression

IPT focuses on the interpersonal context of depression, specifically how symptoms developed and are maintained through interpersonal interactions (Jeffreys and Weersing 2014). Treatment builds skills to reduce current depression and to improve interpersonal functioning. IPT involves three primary steps: (1) identifying a social problem area linked with the depression, (2) developing effective communication and problem-solving skills to address the social problem, and (3) building, practicing, and applying skills in and out of session (Mufson and Sills 2006). Individual IPT (originally developed for adults) is *well established* to treat adolescent depression (Mufson et al. 1999). Treatment components of IPT include the following:

*Psychoeducation.*    Treatment begins with psychoeducation for the adolescent and parent(s) about clinical depression and their roles in treatment. The therapist explains the nature of depression, with a particular focus on how negative interpersonal processes and events impact and maintain depression. Psychoeducation also includes the therapist explaining the likelihood of improvement and recovery (Mufson and Sills 2006).

*Problem area identification.*    A problem area linked with the depression is identified by conducting an interpersonal inventory. This review of the adolescent's relationships focuses on current relationships, but also covers past relationships, and identifies patterns within the relationships that are most related to the onset and maintenance of depression. The problem area is set as the focus of treatment by the therapist and adolescent (Mufson and Sills 2006).

*Affect identification.*    Depressed adolescents often have difficulty understanding and expressing their emotions as well as understanding their emotions in an interpersonal context. Adolescents may keep negative feelings to themselves or express their feelings in an impulsive or negative manner. Affect identification helps the adolescents recognize their emotions, express their emotions to themselves or others, monitor their emotions, and develop an understanding of the connection between feelings and interpersonal conflict (Jacobson and Mufson 2010).

*Reviewing the symptoms.*    Throughout treatment, adolescents' depressive symptoms are reviewed in order to track progress and to assist them in linking their emotions to events.

*Interpersonal skills.*    The therapist and adolescent work together to learn interpersonal skills and practice these skills/strategies throughout treatment to target the problem area and improve interpersonal functioning. Specific techniques include communication analysis, decision analysis, role playing, and work at home (Mufson and Sills 2006).

*Communication analysis.*    The adolescent is frequently asked to share and review problematic interpersonal events. The therapist and adolescent evaluate how the adolescent could have communicated more effectively to change the outcome of the interaction and the feelings of everyone involved in the event (Mufson and Sills 2006).

*Decision analysis.*    Decision analysis allows the adolescent to develop problem-solving skills. The adolescent considers possible solutions or actions that can be taken, evaluates the advantages and disadvantages of each, and identifies which option to implement first.

*Role playing.*    Role playing may also be used to practice implementing the solutions (Klomek and Mufson 2006). Role playing is an active technique that allows the adolescent and therapist to practice implementing new strategies in a safe environment. The adolescent can explore how to have interpersonal interactions and how to handle difficult interpersonal interactions (Mufson and Sills 2006). The therapist can first model how to successfully implement interpersonal skills and decision-making strategies and also provide feedback to the adolescent during and after the role play (Klomek and Mufson 2006).

*Illustrative Example of IPT*

Individual IPT is *well established* to treat adolescent depression (Mufson et al. 1999). Interpersonal Psychotherapy for Depressed Adolescents (IPT-A) (Mufson et al. 2004) is based on the original IPT model and developed specifically for adolescents. IPT-A is considered at least *probably efficacious* (David-Ferdon and Kaslow 2008).

*Interpersonal psychotherapy for depressed adolescents.*    IPT-A is an individual treatment program for adolescents aged 12 to 18 years, delivered over 12 to 15 sessions. The treatment consists of three phases. In the initial phase, symptoms are identified and diagnosed, and psychoeducation about depression is provided to the parent and adolescent. The adolescent is encouraged to engage in activities to improve his or her depressive symptoms while parents are encouraged to be less critical of their child's performance in academics or activities (Jacobson and Mufson 2010). A target problem is selected from one of four possible areas, including grief (e.g., regarding a death), role transitions (e.g., changing schools, parents divorcing, entering puberty), interpersonal role disputes (e.g., conflict with friends, parents, or siblings), and interpersonal deficits (e.g., social isolation; Klomek and Mufson 2006).

The second phase of treatment identifies and implements strategies to resolve the problem area (Mufson and Sills 2006). The therapist encourages the adolescent to express feelings and to identify connections between feelings and the problem area. Other techniques include communication analysis, role playing, and interpersonal experiments (Mufson and Sills 2006).

The third phase is focused on preparation for termination and independence from the therapist. The therapist works to solidify the adolescent's self-confidence and competence in solving future problems with his or her new interpersonal skills (Jacobson and Mufson 2010). The adolescent and therapist identify potential warning signs for recurrence of depression and develop ideas about how to maintain treatment gains. The parent also may be involved in a final session to review the adolescent's progress, strategies learned, warning signs of relapse, and to discuss any potential future treatment directions (Mufson and Sills 2006). See Table 4.1 for a summary of evidence based psychosocial treatments for youth.

Table 4.1 Evidence-Based Psychosocial Treatments for Youth

| | Treatment | Manual | Age | Format | Year | Authors | Price | URL for download or purchase |
|---|---|---|---|---|---|---|---|---|
| IPT | IPT-A | Interpersonal Psychotherapy for Depressed Adolescents, Second Edition | Adolescent | Individual | 2004 | Mufson, Dorta, Moreau, and Weissman | $32.00 Paperback, $77.00 hardcover | http://www.guilford.com/books/Interpersonal-Psychotherapy-for-Depressed-Adolescents/Mufson-Dorta-Moreau-Weissman/9781609182267 |
| CBT | ACTION | Treating Depressed Youth: Therapist Manual for 'ACTION' | Child | Group | 2007 | Stark, Schnoebelen, Simpson, Hargrave, Molnar and Glen | $24.00 | http://www.workbook publishing.com/treating-depressed-youth-therapist-manual-for-action.html |
| | STAR-Center | Cognitive Therapy Treatment Manual for Depressed and Suicidal Youth | Adolescent | Individual | 1997 | Brent and Poling | Free download or $10.00 | https://www.starcenter.pitt.edu/Download-Manuals/18/Default.aspx |
| | CWD-A | Leader's Manual for Adolescent Groups: Adolescent Coping with Depression Course | Adolescent | Group | 1990 | Clarke, Lewinsohn, and Hops | Free download | https://research.kpchr.org/Research/Research-Areas/Mental-Health/Youth-Depression-Programs#Downloads |
| | TADS | Treatment for Adolescents with Depression Study (TADS) Cognitive Behavior Therapy Manual | Adolescent | Group | 2006 | Curry, Wells, Brent, Clarke, Rohde, Albano, Reinecke, Benazon, and March | Free download | http://tads.dcri.org/tads-manuals |

# Psychotropic Medication

As described, use of medication to treat depressed youth is on the rise. Most treated youth are seen by physicians and receive some form of medication. With little doubt, most clinicians will find themselves working with youth already under the care of a physician and being treated with medication. The following section provides a brief primer for practitioners.

Of all major classes of medications, selective serotonin reuptake inhibitors (SSRIs) are the only type of antidepressant shown to be efficacious for youth and are considered the "frontline" treatment for pediatric depression (Wagner 2005). Although the exact mechanism of action of SSRIs is unknown, it is believed that SSRIs work by blocking the reuptake of the neurotransmitter serotonin, increasing the concentration of serotonin in the synaptic cleft (Whitaker 2015). Since serotonin is hypothesized to play a role in regulating diverse functions including mood, appetite, and sleep (all of which are implicated in depression), it is thought that such increases in serotonin concentrations may relieve depressive symptoms (Naughton, Mulrooney and Leonard 2000).

Overall, research finds that SSRIs are statistically superior to placebo, though effect size differences are small (Vitiello et al. 2011). This may, in part, be due to the high placebo response rates found for youth (Vitiello et al. 2011). Regarding specific SSRIs, fluoxetine (Prozac), sertraline (Zoloft), citalopram (Celexa), and escitalopram (Lexipro) have been found to be statistically more effective in treating child/adolescent depression compared with placebo (Emslie et al. 2009; Findling, Robb, and Bose 2013; Wagner 2005; Wagner et al. 2006). Of note, however, results regarding the effectiveness of citalopram are mixed. One RCT found evidence for the effectiveness of citalopram (Wagner et al. 2004), whereas another did not (von Knorring et al. 2006). Of the effective SSRIs, only two are Food and Drug Administration (FDA)-approved for the treatment of pediatric depression: fluoxetine (Prozac) (for ages 8 to 17 years) and escitalopram (Lexapro) (for ages 12 to 17 years).

Other drugs have been evaluated. Evidence for effectiveness has *not* been found for paroxetine (Paxil), venlafaxine ER (Effexor XR), mirtzapine (Remeron), or tricyclic antidepressants in youth samples (Wagner 2005). To date, bupropion (Wellbutrin) has not been examined with children and adolescents (Wagner 2005). See Table 4.2 for a summary of pharmacological treatment options for youth depression.

*Table 4.2 Pharmacological Treatment for Youth Depression*

| Drug | Brand name | FDA approved? | Approved for | Class | Proposed mechanism of action |
|---|---|---|---|---|---|
| Fluoxetine | Prozac | X | 8–17 years | SSRI | Blocks reuptake of serotonin |
| Sertraline | Zoloft | | | SSRI | Blocks reuptake of serotonin |
| Escitalopram | Lexapro | X | 12–17 years | SSRI | Blocks reuptake of serotonin |
| Citalopram | Celexa | | | SSRI | Blocks reuptake of serotonin |

### Medication in Combination with CBT

Although the widely held belief that the combination of medication and CBT may be superior to each treatment alone (i.e., more treatment is better treatment) is logical, evidence supporting use of combined treatment over monotherapy is somewhat mixed (Vitiello 2009). The Treatment of Adolescent Depression Study (March et al. 2004) demonstrated that combined treatment resulted in superior treatment gains compared to fluoxetine or CBT alone after 12 weeks. In the longer term, however, combined treatment had similar outcomes as compared to monotherapies as outcomes for all three groups (combination, medication alone, CBT alone) converged by week 24 for rate of response and by week 30 for reduction of depression symptoms. Additionally, the Treatment of Resistant Depression in Adolescents (TORDIA) study (Brent et al. 2008) evaluated a second-step intervention (switch to a different SSRI or SSRI plus CBT) for adolescents who did not improve initially with SSRI treatment, finding that CBT may add to the effectiveness of SSRIs. Results indicated higher response rates for those receiving medication plus CBT as compared to those receiving medication alone. In contrast, however, clinician and participant ratings of depression did not differ between groups.

Similarly, Kennard and colleagues (2014) assessed whether initial antidepressant treatment responders differentially benefited from continued fluoxetine versus continued fluoxetine plus CBT, finding mixed benefits to combined treatment. The fluoxetine-only group did not differ significantly from the fluoxetine plus CBT group in time to remission, though youth who received combined treatment had lower rates of relapse and longer time to relapse than those receiving medication-only by week 30. In addition, the combination group received a significantly lower maximum daily dose of fluoxetine than the medication-only group, suggesting that adding CBT following initial response to fluoxetine may lower medication dosage needs while achieving similar or superior outcomes as compared to medication alone.

### Suicide Risk

Much of the discussion around medication for youth depression has focused on safety issues related to suicide risk. In response to concerns about antidepressant treatment and suicide, the FDA convened a panel of suicide experts to review trials of antidepressant treatment for children and adolescents. Wagner (2005) summarized the findings, noting that the risk of suicidality (ideation and behavior) was reported to be 4 percent in individuals taking medication as compared to 2 percent for those treated with placebo. The greatest risk appeared to be during the first couple of months of treatment. It is important to note that there have been no deaths by suicide in any medication trial and that research indicates that antidepressant use is not associated with increased risk for suicide in patients with MDD (see Hammad, Laughren, and Racoosin 2006 for a review of 207 trials). Nevertheless, the panel concluded that a "black-box warning" (i.e., text appearing on the prescription drug label to call attention to potential serious risks) was warranted (Wagner 2005).

The American Psychological Association (APA) and American Academy of Child and Adolescent Psychiatry (AACAP) expressed concern that the black-box warning may not be consistent with research and may lead some youth to go untreated (Wagner 2005). Indeed, decreases were observed in diagnoses of depression, depression-related office visits resulting in prescriptions, and use of SSRIs in youth. These decreases in use of medication occurred at the same time that the number of suicides actually increased (Olfson et al. 2013; Seedat 2014).

Although there is no evidence that antidepressants increase risk for suicide in youth, it is unclear whether antidepressants reduce risk for suicide.

In the Treatment for Adolescents with Depression Study (TADS), the fluoxetine-only group showed higher rates of suicidality than all other treatment
groups (including CBT plus fluoxetine), though no completed suicides were
recorded in any group (March et al. 2004). This suggests that the addition
of CBT may protect against suicidality in patients taking fluoxetine. However, risk of suicidality was not lower in the CBT plus medication group
compared to medication alone in the TORDIA study (Brent et al. 2008).

### Conclusions Regarding Antidepressant Treatment

In conclusion, evidence of effectiveness has been found for SSRIs in treating adolescent depression [fluoxetine (Prozac), sertraline (Zoloft), escitalopram (Lexapro), and citalopram (Celexa)], though findings for citalopram
are mixed. Integrated CBT plus medication may lead to faster response
(March et al. 2004) and lower necessary doses (Kennard et al. 2014); however, combined treatment appears to result in similar gains to CBT alone
in the long term (e.g., March et al. 2007; TADS Team et al. 2009).

Importantly, despite widespread use of pharmaceuticals, one-third of
treated youth do not experience full remission of their depressive symptoms when prescribed antidepressant medication (Vitiello et al. 2011). In
addition, unpleasant side effects, questions regarding potential increases in
risk of relapse (Kirsch 2014), and hypothesized long-term brain changes
(Whitaker 2015) raise questions about the balance of benefit and risk. What
is more, concerns of publication biases of RCTs (i.e., only positive results
are disseminated) have been raised, potentially inflating estimates of antidepressant effectiveness (Leventhal and Antonuccio 2009). Further complicating the issue of antidepressant use, the mechanism of action responsible
for SSRIs remains unclear. Additional research examining the long-term
effectiveness and safety of pharmaceutical interventions for child/adoles-
cent depression is clearly needed. Thus, caution may be warranted when
considering antidepressant medication as a treatment option for youth.

# Putting It All Together

Best practice guidelines exist and may be helpful for future reference.
These guidelines come from the National Institute for Health and Clinical

Excellence (2013; UK, https://www.nice.org.uk/guidance/qs48), AACAP (Birmaher, Brent, and AACAP Work Group on Quality Issues 2007; Birmaher, Brent, and Benson 1998), and the Texas Children's Medication Algorithm Project (Hughes et al. 2007).

Kaslow and colleagues also have accumulated helpful suggestions when approaching treatment for child or adolescent depression (David-Ferdon and Kaslow 2008; Kaslow et al. 2014). For example, it is essential to:

- Start with a comprehensive assessment
- Attend to developmental level, gender, and culture
- Include family where relevant, possible, and appropriate
- Target comorbid conditions
- Closely monitor youth treated with antidepressants for worsening symptoms, suicidality, manic switching, and distress.

In terms of treatment selection, youth's age (child or adolescent) and the conceptualization of distress may help to guide choice of intervention from among evidence-based treatments. For instance, an adolescent whose interpersonal relationships appear central to her depression may benefit from IPT. Finally, there is an important need to consider maintenance treatment and relapse prevention. Kennard and colleagues (2006) note that 40 to 70 percent of youth who receive medication or psychosocial treatment experience depression relapse or recurrence, and risk for relapse is highest within the first year following treatment. Direct discussion of relapse prevention strategies in the termination phase of treatment and/or scheduling of booster sessions after formal treatment has ended may help to address these high rates.

# CHAPTER 5

# Case Studies

This chapter includes two case vignettes (one child, one adolescent) to highlight aspects of diagnosis, conceptualization, assessment, and treatment discussed in earlier chapters. The first case focuses on an 11-year-old male with depression and conduct problems, treated with an adaptation of the ACTION program (cognitive-behavioral therapy). The second case involves a 14-year-old female with depression and peer problems, treated with Interpersonal Psychotherapy for Depressed Adolescents (IPT-A).

## Case #1: Luis

---

### LUIS

- 11-year-old male
- Moved to US from Puerto Rico
- Close to maternal grandmother
- Academic and conduct problems
- Difficulties in relations with peers and teachers
- Depressive symptoms

---

Luis is an 11-year-old, Puerto Rican male. He moved to Florida from Puerto Rico approximately 4 years ago, when he was in the second grade. He was accompanied to the United States by his biological mother and father, older brother, younger sister, and maternal grandmother. Luis has an aunt, uncle, and two male cousins who live in Philadelphia, but they do not visit often. The family left behind many extended family members in Puerto Rico.

All six family members live together in a four-bedroom home. Luis shares a bedroom with his brother; his sister, parents, and grandmother occupy the other three bedrooms. Luis is an English language learner, as are his parents and siblings. His grandmother speaks only Spanish, and family members speak primarily Spanish at home. Luis and his grandmother are especially close, and he frequently helps her with daily living, including serving as her primary interpreter.

> *Conceptualization:* Loss of extended family support, a new country and new language, and an interruption in regular pleasant events (baseball) may have contributed to Luis' initial distress.

In Puerto Rico, Luis struggled with academics but excelled socially. His grades were average to below average, and teachers initially suspected a learning disability. A school-based assessment did not suggest evidence of a learning disability, but the evaluator did note that Luis exhibited subclinical attention problems (e.g., difficulty concentrating, trouble sitting still). Luis had many friends and enjoyed playing baseball in a local youth league. Teachers described him as affable and charismatic.

In the fall of second grade, after being in Florida for 2 months, Luis began exhibiting irritability, anger, and conduct problems. Luis was aggressive with other children at recess, had a bad temper, and picked a few fights with other boys. He also had difficulty bonding with authority figures and following rules. He frequently walked away from teachers when being reprimanded and once flooded a school bathroom by placing too much paper in one of the toilets. Luis did make one close friend, Peter, who also had behavioral issues. Luis and Peter were often caught getting into trouble together.

Within the last year, Luis' problems at school became much worse. He stopped turning in homework and refused to do in-class work. He was also suspended from school for fighting. The school referred him to the school counselor, who referred him for therapy. His family, who attends church regularly, visited a pastoral counselor who also suggested treatment. Luis' irritability continued to

> *Current practice:* School staff, clergy, and physicians are often among the first to recommend therapy.

increase, and he began to report somatic problems like stomach pain and headaches. Once an avid baseball player, Luis now preferred to stay in his room playing video games. His parents also noticed that Luis had put on some weight over the last few months. They visited Luis' pediatrician, who also suggested Luis may benefit from psychotherapy. Luis' parents were unsure whether or not Luis needed therapy. While his behavior at school continued to decline, they did not notice any problematic behavior at home, apart from decreased physical activity. Luis' grandmother was very opposed to Luis receiving therapy, stating that Luis did not have a problem. His parents finally called a therapist when Luis became frustrated, yelled at his grandmother, and threw a bowl at her during dinner.

Luis' mother and father accompanied him to his first appointment with a child therapist at a community mental health care clinic. They explained Luis' history of problems at school and his recent outburst in the home. The therapist discussed that the next sessions would focus on assessing Luis' problem areas in more detail, for the purposes of identifying an appropriate diagnosis and treatment. Then the focus would shift to intervention, which would involve working with Luis as well as the adults in his family.

## Assessment

From the initial session, it was clear to the therapist that Luis was very close with his grandmother. As such, she thought that obtaining the grandmother's perspective, in addition to the parents' perspectives, was important. She set up a meeting in which she met with all three adults. The therapist learned that Luis' father was primarily responsible for discipline but also that he was often away from home for work. Luis' mother reported feeling helpless to control Luis' behavior. She said, "Nothing I do works. Yelling, ignoring, bribing; nothing." Interestingly, while Luis' parents expressed distress at his increasingly problematic behavior at home (e.g., fighting with siblings), the grandmother reported that she did not see a problem. She described him as a sweet boy who helps her tremendously with household tasks and communication. The therapist decided to complete the Kiddie Schedule for Affective Disorders and Schizophrenia— Present and Lifetime version (K-SADS-PL) using all three adults as informants, noting discrepancies as they occurred. Luis' parents reported academic problems, somatic problems, and conduct problems, while Luis' grandmother reported only somatic issues.

The therapist also met individually with Luis. She noticed that during the initial session, Luis appeared upset but was silent while his parents did most of the talking. When meeting alone with Luis, he exhibited similar behavior. For instance, when she asked questions about how he had been feeling, he was silent or said, "I don't know; you tell me." She decided to spend the majority of one session talking to Luis about baseball, which he was able to discuss at length. They continued to make small talk at the beginning of sessions as a way to maintain this initial connection. Once rapport was established, she completed the K-SADS-PL with Luis as well. He reported academic and behavioral problems but also a great deal of depressive symptoms and interpersonal problems of which the therapist had been previously unaware.

Additionally, the therapist obtained parental consent to obtain Luis' school records and to speak with Luis' counselor and classroom teacher. Over the next week, the therapist obtained the school records and spoke with the counselor and teacher via phone. The therapist learned that Luis was frequently tardy and absent from school because of illness, and that he had received multiple in-school suspensions, in addition to the out-of-school suspension reported by Luis' parents. The counselor said that she had a very difficult time engaging Luis in conversation, and the classroom teacher described him as a "troublemaker who can't get along with other kids."

## Conceptualization and Diagnosis

The therapist conceptualized that Luis' move to Florida from Puerto Rico was likely the impetus for his conduct problems and depressive symptoms. The move was very stressful on Luis and his family, and this stress was perpetuated by Luis' lack of connection to teachers, peers, and pleasant activities in his new home. The therapist further hypothesized that the parents' differential discipline styles, as well as the grandmother's discrepant views on Luis' issues, may be maintaining some of his behavior problems. On the basis of her assessment, the therapist diagnosed Luis with major depressive

*Assessment:* Monitoring treatment progress does not have to be time-consuming or overly burdensome for the therapist or the family. The therapist may choose to administer a measure before session and may also ask family members to track symptoms at home.

disorder and conduct disorder. She elected to utilize the Child Depression Inventory 2 (CDI 2) to monitor progress and administered it every 2 weeks during treatment. She also asked Luis' mother to track the frequency of Luis' problems at school and conflicts at home.

## Treatment

The therapist reviewed treatments that could incorporate Luis' caregivers in addressing his difficulties. She found a helpful chapter that articulated how the ACTION program may be modified for use with individual children (Stark, Streusand, Arora, and Patel 2011) and learned that it had been adapted for use with boys 9 to 14 years of age (Stark et al. 2011a), including a parent training manual (Stark, Yancy, Schnoebelen, Hargrave, and Molnar, 2011). The therapist met with Luis, his parents, and his grandmother for one session, in which the treatment rationale was explained.

Therapy occurred weekly over a period of 4 months. Luis attended each session with his mother, and the therapist scheduled additional meetings or phone consultations with Luis' mother to relay parent-specific information.

*Treatment:* A group treatment program, such as ACTION, can be modified for an individual therapy setting. In this case, information from the parenting group was relayed to caregivers over the phone or in brief, separate meetings.

Each ACTION session follows roughly the same structure, with specific content changing as therapy progresses. Sessions begin with a short period (e.g., 5 minutes) of unstructured time to build and maintain rapport. Next, the therapist sets the agenda and checks in regarding progress toward established goals. Homework from the previous session is reviewed. The bulk of the session is focused on a coping skills activity and skill building. The therapist ends session by reviewing the child's positive behaviors for the purposes of reinforcement (praise) and shaping of new behavior. Finally, homework is assigned for the upcoming week.

The early sessions involving *affective education* were important for Luis and his mother to have a common language with which to discuss

---

## Action Components

- Affective Education (3 Bs)
- Goal Setting
- Coping Skills Training
- Problem-Solving Training (5 Ps)
- Cognitive Restructuring
- Building a Positive Sense of Self

---

Luis's depression and the connections between his body, brain, and behavior (3 Bs). They both learned that Luis was often feeling sad internally, although he exhibited irritability and acted out. For example, Luis described feeling "tight, like I might explode" along with having the thought "Everyone hates me," which led him to withdraw from or, alternately, act aggressively toward peers. *Goal setting* helped to clarify the direction of intervention. Luis set two goals for himself: to improve his behavior at school and to play baseball again. His mother also set two goals for herself: to improve her management of Luis' behavior and to increase positive interactions in the family. Luis particularly enjoyed the *coping skills training* section of treatment (roughly sessions 2 to 9). He had a great deal of energy, and the active nature of the coping skills curriculum appeared to fit well with his temperament. It also provided a catalyst for Luis to work toward one of his goals, to play baseball again. Luis' mother implemented a sticker chart to reward Luis' positive behavior, and Luis also was excited by the prospect of earning rewards, such as a movie night.

After several weeks of gradual improvement in behavioral activation and decreases in CDI 2 scores, as well as consistently high levels of engagement from Luis and his mother, Luis stopped doing his therapy homework. When she inquired about this, she discovered that Luis' grandmother may be inadvertently undermining some of the work Luis was doing in therapy. For example, Luis' mother reported that the grandmother was rewarding Luis with stickers without evidence of the goal behavior and that she let Luis skip his after-school baseball practice on a few occasions to get ice cream with her instead. The therapist thought it best to address parenting issues with the mother (as opposed to involving the grandmother directly in treatment) as a way to empower her and not invite triangulation of family members in session.

The therapist encouraged Luis' mother to take primary control of managing Luis' reinforcements (sticker chart) and pleasant events scheduling (baseball practice). The therapist noticed, however, that Luis' behavior did not improve; rather, the family reported increased conflict, especially between Luis' mother and grandmother. Luis' mother described that the house felt "hostile, like we're all in different camps."

The therapist realized that she may have neglected to address the important dynamic Luis has with his grandmother and the importance of grandparenting in Luis' culture. She invited the grandmother to attend sessions in an effort to address this more directly. Luis' grandmother and mother

*Conceptualization:* It is important to consider the child's difficulties in cultural context, where relevant. In this case, the therapist's initial intervention conflicted with the family culture and structure, causing more conflict and interfering with treatment.

worked together to establish common expectations for reinforcing Luis' behavior and to carve out special time Luis could spend with his grandmother in addition to attending baseball practice. The therapist further encouraged Luis' father to phone into sessions when possible so that he, too, could participate. The adults in the family exhibited more consistency in their responses to Luis' behavior, and Luis was able to practice problem-solving skills (learned in sessions 5 to 9) in situations involving disagreements with family members. Over time, the family appeared much more cohesive and reported continued decreases in Luis' problem behavior.

At this point in treatment, Luis' depressive symptoms and behavior had improved enough for him to fully delve and engage into the *cognitive restructuring* (sessions 10 to 20) aspect of the ACTION program. The therapist discovered that Luis held a number of negative beliefs about himself and often misattributed hostile intent to others (especially peers), which precipitated aggressive behavior. Luis liked the idea of talking back to his "Muck Monster," the internal generator of negative thoughts. Externalization of his negative thoughts was particularly important in helping to build

> *Treatment:* Cognitive restructuring is typically introduced later in treatment, once the child and family fully understand the treatment rationale, behavioral activation is in place, and some coping skills have been established.

Luis' *positive sense of self* (a focus of sessions 12 to 20). He said that he felt relieved that he was not "crazy for having these weird thoughts."

## Outcomes

Near the end of treatment, Luis' CDI 2 scores had declined significantly, placing him below clinically significant cutoff scores. His mother's report of the frequency of school problems also decreased, and family fighting had not been reported for several weeks. In conjunction with Luis and his parents, the therapist introduced the idea of termination. Several sessions were spent reinforcing what Luis and his family had learned and preparing for future difficulties (e.g., transition to middle school). The therapist scheduled two booster sessions spaced 1 and 2 months after the final therapy session. During these sessions, the therapist checked in with the family regarding Luis' progress and helped to problem-solve around minor issues that presented themselves in the interim.

## Action Resources

- Stark, Kevin D., William Streusand, Prerna Arora, and Puja Patel. 2011. "Childhood Depression: The ACTION Treatment Program." In *Child and Adolescent Therapy: Cognitive-Behavioral Procedure,* 4th ed., edited by Philip C. Kendall, 190–233. New York, NY: Guilford Press.
- Stark, Kevin D., Sarah Schnoebelen, Jennifer Hargrave, Johanna Molnar, and Rand Glen. 2011. *'ACTION' Workbook:*

*Cognitive-Behavioral Therapy for Treating Depressed Boys.*
Ardmore, PA: Workbook Publishing.
- Stark, Kevin D., Mary G. Yancy, Sarah Schnoebelen, Jennifer
  Hargrave, and Johanna Molnar. 2011. *'ACTION' Workbook
  for Parents of Depressed Boys.* Workbook Publishing. Treatment
  manuals available from: www.workbookpublishing.com
  /depression.html

## Case #2: Alyssa

### ALYSSA

- 15-year-old female
- Former ballet dancer
- School transition
- Peer victimization
- New conflicts with mother
- Depressive symptoms

Alyssa is a 15-year-old Caucasian female living in a suburban community in Illinois. Her parents divorced when she was 8 years old, and she has lived with her mother since. Alyssa and her mother are very close, and they enjoy spending time together cooking and taking evening walks. She and her father, who she sees every other weekend, have a close relationship, but she describes him as somewhat shy and introverted. She is an only child.

Alyssa has always been very athletic. She especially enjoyed dance classes and was recruited to train at a prestigious ballet school at the age of 6 years. She took classes 4 days a week and formed a tight-knit group of friends. They often had sleepovers at each other's houses, and they called themselves the "ballet family." When she was 13 years of age, Alyssa suffered a knee injury that sidelined her training for several months. On the advice of doctors, Alyssa significantly cut back on training to recover. Once she healed, Alyssa felt that she had missed too much time and lost too much strength to be able to keep up, and she left the intensive ballet program.

*Conceptualization:* Role transitions are common in adolescence but, at times, may present emotional challenges. Alyssa faced a role transition away from ballet and into a new school on top of normative developmental changes, such as increasing autonomy.

When Alyssa started high school the next year, she reported feeling lost. She no longer felt the support of her close friends, who continued to train without her. She also was faced with making new friends at a much larger school. Given that she had spent so much time with dance, she had not developed other interests. She said she felt like she was "the only one at school without something to do after school." Her mother encouraged her to try out for the school's dance team, but Alyssa felt self-conscious about her body and was afraid to dance again. Alyssa's mother also suggested she reach out to her old friends. Alyssa felt uncomfortable about this too, as she had not spoken to them in many months. With support from her mother, she sent her old friends an online message, posted to their private "Ballet Family" Facebook group page.

*Conceptualization:* Friendships typically provide youth with social and emotional support. Alyssa, however, had to face the loss of several friends as well as relational aggression from and victimization by these peers.

Unfortunately, Alyssa received a very negative response from her former peer group. They deleted her from their private Facebook group and began posting cruel messages and taunting photos on her personal Facebook page. For example, they posted that "Fat ballerinas can't wear pink tights" and a picture of the group hanging out with the caption, "Wish you were here! NOT." Alyssa was devastated. She withdrew, spending a majority of her day in her room and online, looking at the Facebook pages of her former friends. She ate and slept less, and, in a short period of time, her grades significantly declined.

Alyssa's mother noticed the change in Alyssa and set up an appointment with her pediatrician, who screened Alyssa for depression. Alyssa's score on the depression screener exceeded clinically significant cutoff levels, and the pediatrician recommended that Alyssa begin taking a low dose of fluoxetine (Prozac). She also recommended Alyssa receive individual therapy. She was referred to a local group practice and placed on a waiting list to see a therapist. After 5 weeks, Alyssa and her mother both noticed that Alyssa was sleeping and eating better but that she continued to feel sad and ruminate about her old friends.

> *Conceptualization:* It can be difficult for both adolescents and parents to navigate adolescents' increasing autonomy. Conflict may arise when parents and adolescents have different ideas and expectations about the degree of autonomy adolescents should be granted.

At this time, Alyssa also began to isolate herself from her mother, with whom she typically felt comfortable talking and spending time. She often argued with her mother, becoming especially upset when she felt her mother was telling her what to do. Alyssa's grades continued to decline, to the point where the school counselor called her mother to express concern that Alyssa may not pass the ninth grade. Alyssa's mother was shocked and called the group practice to inquire about the current availability for counseling. An appointment was made for the following week, and Alyssa attended her first therapy session with her mother. The therapist observed Alyssa to be depressed but agreeable, conscientious, and warm.

### Assessment

During the first session, the therapist asked both Alyssa and her mother to discuss the history of Alyssa's struggles. He noted that both parties agreed that Alyssa had been feeling depressed but that Alyssa's mother seemed more concerned with Alyssa's lack of participation in the school dance team and with the increasing conflict between mother and daughter than did Alyssa. The therapist, Alyssa, and Alyssa's mother decided together that formal diagnostic assessment would occur primarily with Alyssa but that the therapist also would interview her mother separately in an effort to gain an additional perspective. Alyssa completed the Center for Epidemiologic Studies of Depression-Revised (CESD-R), and her scores were significantly elevated above the clinical threshold. Given that Alyssa had discussed extreme self-consciousness in social settings, as well as body dissatisfaction, the therapist decided to administer the Diagnostic Interview Schedule for Children (DISC-IV) to assess for depression as well as possible comorbidities, such as anxiety and/or eating issues.

As part of this process, the therapist inquired about the presence of suicidality. During her interview with the therapist, Alyssa's mother denied that Alyssa had ever had any suicidal thinking. However, Alyssa alone disclosed that she experienced near-daily suicidal ideation. Alyssa's disclosures surprised the therapist, given Alyssa's generally agreeable demeanor and her mother's report. The therapist and Alyssa met with Alyssa's mother to discuss the suicidal ideation. Together they developed a plan for ongoing assessment and risk management. Specifically, Alyssa agreed to address suicidality in treatment and to disclose should her ideation increase or should she develop plans and/or intent to harm herself. Alyssa said she was initially "terrified to admit" that she had suicidal thoughts but that disclosing to the therapist and to her mother "felt like a huge weight off my shoulders." Alyssa's mother said she also felt relieved to know about her daughter's thoughts, although she expressed significant concern that the antidepressant medication "caused Alyssa to be suicidal." The therapist reviewed basic information about the link between antidepressant use and youth suicidality and recommended that the family consult with their prescribing pediatrician about their concerns.

> *Assessment:* In this case, assessing for suicidality resulted in identification of an important target of treatment. It also appears to have resulted in Alyssa feeling heard and supported by both her mother and the therapist.

## Conceptualization and Diagnosis

The therapist conceptualized that Alyssa's depression stemmed primarily from difficulty with role transitions. He felt that Alyssa, having been separated from an activity that formed the foundation for her peer support system, had experienced a significant disruption in her interpersonal context. This disruption was exacerbated by her peers' cruel treatment and excommunication from the group. As a result, she experienced conflict, isolation, and eventually depression. She struggled to find new activities and friends in part because of feelings of low self-efficacy. At the same time, Alyssa was dealing with typical development issues, such as nego-tiating increasing independence and autonomy from her mother as she transitioned away from childhood and into adolescence. During a time of increased distress and vulnerability (related to peer problems), Alyssa found these more normative struggles of adolescence to be particularly difficult to navigate. The therapist conceptualized that increased mother–daughter conflict stemmed primarily from this tension.

Taken together with Alyssa's CESD-R score, results of the DISC-IV indicated that Alyssa indeed met criteria for major depressive disorder. Although she endorsed some symptoms of social anxiety and disordered eating, these symptoms did not rise to the threshold of comorbid di-agnoses. Given his conceptualization of the origin and maintenance of Alyssa's depression as interpersonal in nature, the therapist elected to use IPT-A and to administer the CESD-R once per month as a way to track progress.

### Treatment

At the outset of therapy, the therapist discussed issues related to confi-dentiality in working with adolescents. He explained to Alyssa and her mother that, while Alyssa was a minor, it may be helpful if Alyssa could feel that some of what she discussed in therapy could be kept private. The therapist explained that he would inform her mother if Alyssa were to disclose any information about abuse, neglect, suicidality, or homi-cidality. Together with the therapist, Alyssa and her mother then negoti-ated whether other topics such as substance use, dating, or sexual activity would be disclosed. The group decided that should any of these issues be impacting Alyssa's health or safety, that Alyssa would inform her mother during session, with the support of the therapist.

In the initial phases of treatment, the therapist provided psychoedu-cation to Alyssa and her mother regarding the symptoms of depression, its relation to interpersonal functioning, and its impact on an individual's ability to complete responsibilities as they may have before. Alyssa was en-couraged to stay as active as possible because withdrawal can worsen de-pression. She then completed an interpersonal inventory with the therapist in which she identified key people in her life who were influential to her mood. She identified her two former best friends from ballet, her mother,

> *Treatment:* Early in IPT-A, the therapist assigns the adolescent the "limited sick role," which helps the youth and parent(s) acknowledge that the youth may not be expected to meet all previous obligations, at least for a time. At the same time, the youth is encouraged to stay as behaviorally active as possible.

and her father. From here, she and the therapist were able to determine that her depression was centrally tied to role transitions, difficulties adjusting to her new life without ballet, and becoming an increasingly autonomous young woman. Alyssa reported that she felt "relieved to figure out what has been going on." She said she knew that losing friends contributed to her depression, but that she had not been aware that the stress associated with developing more autonomy may be impacting her relationship with her mother.

In the middle phase of treatment, Alyssa learned how to label her affect and to express her emotions. She realized that she had a tendency to "keep it all in" and that she believed she should not have or express any negative feelings. She realized that her injury had made her very upset but that she had not allowed herself to express it at the time. The therapist then engaged Alyssa in communication analysis around the early stages of her friendship dissolution. In particular, they discussed how Alyssa's lack of communication with her friends may have contributed to her friends initially feeling confused or alienated. Alyssa noted, "Yeah, I guess I fell off the face of the earth. I'm sure they wondered what was wrong with me." The therapist was careful, however, not to assign blame for the bullying to Alyssa's social withdrawal. The therapist worked with Alyssa in processing her grief around losing her friends. Alyssa also was able to practice effective communication with her mother via role-playing. The

## IPT-A Components

- Symptom identification and diagnosis
- Psychoeducation
- Target problem identification
- Problem resolution skills
- Preparation for termination

therapist brought her mother into session to work through a particularly contentious issue, Alyssa's lack of extracurricular activities.

Around this time, Alyssa began to report that she felt "lighter, more energetic." She told the therapist that, after meeting with the pediatrician, she and her mother had decided that she would slowly come off of her medication. The therapist encouraged Alyssa and her mother to continue to be in contact with her pediatrician who could monitor the tapering, and Alyssa's mother agreed to schedule a check-in appointment. Alyssa also was able to identify an extracurricular activity that she would like to try: joining the high school yearbook staff. As part of a series of therapy homework assignments, Alyssa was able to take the necessary steps to secure a place on the yearbook staff.

The final phase of therapy, the termination phase, involved Alyssa discussing and preparing for termination with the therapist. She was able to express her anxiety about ending therapy, as well as her pride that she had been able to work through her depression by processing difficult interpersonal issues. Alyssa's mother joined her for the last three sessions in which they discussed strategies Alyssa could use to deal with future challenging situations. They also discussed warning signs that could signal a need for additional therapeutic support.

### Outcomes

By the end of treatment, Alyssa's scores on the CESD-R were in the normal range. She reported feeling much more resolved regarding her transition away from ballet and more excited about her new role on the yearbook staff. She also reported that working through conflicts with her mother using effective communication tools had significantly improved their relationship and had led to her feeling increasingly confident about being more autonomous. She had come completely off of her medication, under her physician's guidance, and was excited to take an upcoming trip to an amusement park with her new friends from the yearbook.

Approximately 6 months later, the therapist received a call from Alyssa's mother, who reported that Alyssa had recently disclosed to her that the depression "was back." Her mother said she thought it may have to do with a situation involving Alyssa's first romantic relationship. Alyssa

> *Treatment:* As depression tends to be chronic, adolescents may benefit from returning to therapy for short periods of time when depression returns. These additional sessions may help youth to review skills previously learned and help to identify areas in which additional skills are needed.

returned for a series of five sessions, in which Alyssa was able to identify that a recent romantic relationship breakup had triggered previous patterns of social withdrawal and poor communication, leading to complications in her relationships with friends, and resulting feelings of depression. In reviewing skills learned during the previous course of treatment, Alyssa was able to process her loss of relationship and reimplement positive communication strategies that helped her gain social support during this difficult time.

## IPT-A Resources

- Jacobson, Colleen M., and Laura Mufson. 2010. "Treating Adolescent Depression Using Interpersonal Psychotherapy." In *Evidence-Based Psychotherapies for Children and Adolescents*, edited by John R. Weisz, and Alan E. Kazdin, 140–55. New York, NY: Guilford Press.
- Mufson, Laura H., Kristen Pollack Dorta, Donna Moreau, and Myrna M. Weissman. 2004. *Interpersonal Psychotherapy for Depressed Adolescents*, 2nd ed. New York, NY: The Guilford Press.

# References

Abela, John R. Z., Cristina M. Aydin, and Randy P. Auerbach. 2007. "Responses to Depression in Children: Reconceptualizing the Relation among Response Styles." *Journal of Abnormal Child Psychology* 35 (6): 913–27. doi:10.1007/s10802-007-9143-2.

Abela, John R. Z., Karen Brozina, and Emily P. Haigh. 2002. "An Examination of the Response Styles Theory of Depression in Third- and Seventh-Grade Children: A Short-Term Longitudinal Study." *Journal of Abnormal Child Psychology* 30 (5): 515–27. doi:10.1023/A:1019873015594.

Abela, John R. Z., and Benjamin L. Hankin. 2008. "The Development of Depression During the Transition from Early to Middle Adolescence: A Cognitive Vulnerability-stress Perspective." *Journal of Affective Disorders* 107: S111–2.

Abela, John R. Z., Benjamin L. Hankin, Dana M. Sheshko, Michael B. Fishman, and Darren Stolow. 2012. "Multi-Wave Prospective Examination of the Stress-Reactivity Extension of Response Styles Theory of Depression in High-Risk Children and Early Adolescents." *Journal of Abnormal Child Psychology* 40 (2): 277–87. doi:10.1007/s10802-011-9563-x.

Abela, John R. Z., Maya Sakellaropoulo, and Elizabeth Taxel. 2007. "Integrating Two Subtypes of Depression Psychodynamic Theory and Its Relation to Hopelessness Depression in Early Adolescents." *The Journal of Early Adolescence* 27 (3): 363–85. doi:10.1177/0272431607302004.

Abramson, Lyn Y., Gerald I. Metalsky, and Lauren B. Alloy. 1989. "Hopelessness Depression: A Theory-Based Subtype of Depression." *Psychological Review* 96 (2): 358–72. doi:10.1037/0033-295X.96.2.358.

Abramson, Lyn Y., Martin E. Seligman, and John D. Teasdale. 1978. "Learned Helplessness in Humans: Critique and Reformulation." *Journal of Abnormal Psychology* 87 (1): 49–74. doi:10.1037/0021-843X.87.1.49.

Achenbach, Thomas M., Stephanie H. McConaughy, and Catherine T. Howell. 1987. "Child/Adolescent Behavioral and Emotional Problems: Implications of Cross-Informant Correlations for Situational Specificity." *Psychological Bulletin* 101 (2): 213–32.

Aguilera, M., B. Arias, M. Wichers, N. Barrantes-Vidal, J. Moya, H. Villa, J. van Os, et al. 2009. "Early Adversity and 5-HTT/BDNF Genes: New Evidence of Gene-Environment Interactions on Depressive Symptoms in a General Population." *Psychological Medicine* 39 (9): 1425–32. doi:10.1017/S0033291709005248.

American Psychiatric Association. 2013. *Diagnostic and Statistical Manual of Mental Disorders (DSM-5)*. 5th ed. Washington, DC: American Psychiatric Publishing.

Angold, Adrian, and Elizabeth J. Costello. 2000. "The Child and Adolescent Psychiatric Assessment (CAPA)." *Journal of the American Academy of Child & Adolescent Psychiatry* 39: 39–48. doi:10.1017/S003329170003498X.

Angold, Adrian, and Elizabeth J. Costello. 2001. "The Epidemiology of Depression in Children and Adolescents." In *The Depressed Child and Adolescent*, 2nd ed., edited by Ian M. Goodyer, 143–78. New York, NY: Cambridge University Press.

Angold, Adrian, and Prudence W. Fisher. 1999. "Interviewer-Based Interviews." In *Diagnostic Assessment in Child and Adolescent Psychopathology*, edited by David Shaffer, Lucas P. Christopher, and John E. Richters, 34–64. New York, NY: Guilford Press.

APA Presidential Task Force on Evidence-Based Practice. 2006. "Evidence-Based Practice in Psychology." *American Psychologist* 61 (4): 271–85. doi:10.1037/0003-066X.61.4.271.

Auerbach, Randy P., Moon Ho Ringo Ho, and Judy C. Kim. 2014. "Identifying Cognitive and Interpersonal Predictors of Adolescent Depression." *Journal of Abnormal Child Psychology* 42 (6): 913–24. doi:10.1007/s10802-013-9845-6.

Balazs, Judit, Mónika Miklósi, Ágnes Keresztény, Christina W. Hoven, Vladimir Carli, Camilla Wasserman, Alan Apter, et al. 2013. "Adolescent Subthreshold-depression and Anxiety: Psychopathology, Functional Impairment and Increased Suicide Risk." *Journal of Child Psychology and Psychiatry* 54 (6): 670–77. doi:10.1111/jcpp.12016.

Beck, Judith. 2011. *Cognitive Behavior Therapy: Basics and Beyond*. New York, NY: Guilford Press.

Bhatia, Shaski K., and Subhash C. Bhatia. 2007. "Childhood and Adolescent Depression." *American Family Physician* 75: 73–80.

Birmaher, Boris, David Brent, and AACAP Work Group on Quality Issues. 2007. "Practice Parameter for the Assessment and Treatment of Children and Adolescents with Depressive Disorders." *Journal of the American Academy of Child & Adolescent Psychiatry* 46 (11): 1503–26. doi:10.1097/chi.0b013e318145ae1c.

Birmaher, Boris, David A. Brent, and R. Scott Benson. 1998. "Summary of the Practice Parameters for the Assessment and Treatment of Children and Adolescents with Depressive Disorders." *Journal of the American Academy of Child & Adolescent Psychiatry* 37 (11): 1234–38. doi:10.1097/00004583-199811000-00028.

Birmaher, Boris, Neal D. Ryan, Douglas E. Williamson, David A. Brent, Joan Kaufman, Ronald E. Dahl, Hames Perel, and Beverly Nelson. 1996. "Childhood and Adolescent Depression: A Review of the Past 10 Years, Part I."

*Journal of The American Academy of Child and Adolescent Psychiatry* 35 (11): 1427–39. doi:10.1097/00004583-199611000-00011.

Boivin, Michel, François Poulin, and Frank Vitaro. 1994. "Depressed Mood and Peer Rejection in Childhood." *Development and Psychopathology*, 6: 483–98.

Borelli, Jessica L., and Mitchell J. Prinstein. 2006. "Reciprocal, Longitudinal Associations among Adolescents' Negative Feedback-Seeking, Depressive Symptoms, and Peer Relations." *Journal of Abnormal Child Psychology* 34 (2): 159–69. doi:10.1007/s10802-005-9010-y.

Braet, Caroline, Laura Wante, Marie Lotte Van Beveren, and Lotte Theuwis. 2015. "Is the Cognitive Triad a Clear Marker of Depressive Symptoms in Youngsters?" *European Child and Adolescent Psychiatry* 24 (10): 1261–68. doi:10.1007/s00787-015-0674-8.

Brent, David, Graham Emslie, Greg Clarke, Karen Dineen Wagner, Joan Rosenbaum Asarnow, Marty Keller, Benedetto Vitiello, et al. 2008. "Switching to Another SSRI or to Venlafaxine with or without Cognitive Behavioral Therapy for Adolescents with SSRI-Resistant Depression: The TORDIA Randomized Controlled Trial." *Journal of the American Medical Association* 299 (8): 901–13. doi:10.1001/jama.299.8.901.

Brent, David A., Diane Holder, David Kolko, Boris Birmaher, Marianne Baugher, Claudia Roth, Satish Iyengar, and Barbara A. Johnson. 1997. "A Clinical Psychotherapy Trial for Adolescent Depression Comparing Cognitive, Family, and Supportive Therapy." *Archives of General Psychiatry* 54 (9): 877–85.

Brent, David A., David J. Kolko, Boris Birmaher, and Marianne Baugher. 1998. "Predictors of Treatment Efficacy in a Clinical Trial of Three Psychosocial Treatments for Adolescent Depression." *Journal of the American Academy of Child and Adolescent Psychiatry* 17 (2): 906. doi:10.1097/00004583-199809000-00010.

Brent, David A., and Kim Poling. 1997. *Cognitive Therapy Treatment Manual for Depressed and Suicidal Youth.* Pittsburgh, PA: Services for Teens at Risk (STAR-Center).

Brozina, Karen, and John R. Z. Abela. 2006. "Symptoms of Depression and Anxiety in Children: Specificity of the Hopelessness Theory." *Journal of Clinical Child and Adolescent Psychology, American Psychological Association* 35 (4): 515–27. doi:10.1207/s15374424jccp3504_3.

Buhrmester, Duane, and Wyndol Furman. 1987. "The Development of Companionship and Intimacy." *Child Development* 58 (4): 1101–13.

Calmes, Christine A., and John E. Roberts. 2008. "Rumination in Interpersonal Relationships: Does Co-Rumination Explain Gender Differences in Emotional Distress and Relationship Satisfaction among College Students?" *Cognitive Therapy and Research* 32 (4): 577–90. doi:10.1007/s10608-008-9200-3.

Calvete, Esther, Izaskun Orue, and Benjamin L. Hankin. 2013. "Transactional Relationships among Cognitive Vulnerabilities, Stressors, and Depressive

Symptoms in Adolescence." *Journal of Abnormal Child Psychology* 41 (3): 399–410. doi:10.1007/s10802-012-9691-y.

Cameron, Judy L. 2004. "Interrelationships between Hormones, Behavior, and Affect during Adolescence: Understanding Hormonal, Physical, and Brain Changes Occurring in Association with Pubertal Activation of the Reproductive Axis. Introduction to part III." *Annals of the New York Academy of Sciences* 1021 (1): 110–23.

Cantwell, Deniis P., Peter M. Lewinsohn, Paul Rohde, and John R. Seeley. 1997. "Correspondence Between Adolescent Report and Parent Report of Psychiatric Diagnostic Data." *Journal of the American Academy of Child & Adolescent Psychiatry* 36 (5): 610–9. doi:10.1097/00004583-199705000-00011.

Cashel, Mary Louise. 2002. "Child and Adolescent Psychological Assessment: Current Clinical Practices and the Impact of Managed Care." *Professional Psychology: Research and Practice* 33 (5): 446–53. doi:10.1037/0735-7028.33.5.446.

Caspi, Avshalom, Karen Sugden, Terrie E. Moffitt, Alan Taylor, Ian W Craig, HonaLee Harrington, Joseph McClay, et al. 2003. "Influence of Life Stress on Depression: Moderation by a Polymorphism in the 5-HTT Gene." *Science* 301 (5631): 386–89. doi:10.1002/9780470114735.hawley00624.

Center for Behavioral Health Statistics and Quality, Substance Abuse and Mental Health Services Administration (SAMHSA), U.S. Department of Health and Human Services (HHS). 2015. "*Behavioral Health Trends in the United States: Results From the 2014 National Survey on Drug Use and Health.*" SMA 15-4927, NSDUH Series H-50. www.samhsa.gov/data/

Chambless, Dianne L., Mary J. Baker, Donald H. Baucom, Larry E. Beutler, Karen S. Calhoun, Paul Crits-Christoph, Anthony Daiuto, et al. 1998. "Update on Empirically Validated Therapies, II." *The Clinical Psychologist* 51 (1): 3–16. doi:10.1037/e555332011-003.

Chambless, Dianne L., and Steven D. Hollon. 1998. "Defining Empirically Supported Therapies." *Journal of Consulting and Clinical Psychology* 66 (1): 7–18. doi:10.1037/0022-006X.66.1.7.

Chambless, Dianne. L., William C. Sanderson, Varda Shoham, Suzanne Bennett Johnson, Kenneth S. Pope, Paul Crits-Christoph, Mary Baker, et al. 1996. "An Update on Empirically Validated Therapies." *The Clinical Psychologist* 49 (2): 5–18.

Chorpita, Bruce F, and Eric L Daleiden. 2009. "Mapping Evidence-Based Treatments for Children and Adolescents: Application of the Distillation and Matching Model to 615 Treatments from 322 Randomized Trials." *Journal of Consulting and Clinical Psychology* 77 (3): 566–79. doi:10.1037/a0014565.

Chrisman, Allan, Helen Egger, Scott N. Compton, John Curry, and David B. Goldston. 2006. "Assessment of Childhood Depression." "*Child and Adolescent Mental Health* 11 (2): 111–6. doi:10.1111/j.1475-3588.2006.00395.x.

Chung, Winnie W., and Fristad, Mary A. 2014. "Depressive Disorders in Children." In *Comprehensive Evidence Based Interventions for Children and Adolescents*, edited by Candice A. Alfano and Deborah C. Beidel, 129–45. Hoboken, NJ: John Wiley & Sons Inc.

Clarke, Gregory N., and Lynn L. Debar. 2010. "Group Cognitive-Behavioral Treatment for Adolescent Depression." In *Evidence-Based Psychotherapies for Children and Adolescents*, edited by John R. Weisz, and Alan E. Kazdin, 110–25. New York, NY: Guilford Press.

Clarke, Gregory, Lynn Debar, Frances Lynch, James Powell, John Gale, Elizabeth O'Connor, Evette Ludman, et al. 2005. "A Randomized Effectiveness Trial of Brief Cognitive-Behavioral Therapy for Depressed Adolescents Receiving Antidepressant Medication." *Journal of the American Academy of Child and Adolescent Psychiatry* 44 (9): 888–98. doi:10.1097/01.chi.0000171904.23947.54.

Clarke, Gregory, Peter Lewinsohn, and Hyman Hops. 1990. *Adolescent Coping With Depression Course.* Eugene, OR: Castilia Press.

Cole, David A. 1991. "Preliminary Support for a Competency-Based Model of Depression in Children." *Journal of Abnormal Psychology* 100 (2): 181–90. doi:10.1037/0021-843X.100.2.181.

Cole, David A. 1990. "Relation of Social and Academic Competence to Depressive Symptoms in Childhood." *Journal of Abnormal Psychology* 99 (4): 422–29. doi:10.1037/0021-843X.99.4.422.

Cole, David A., Scott E. Maxwell, Joan M. Martin, Lachlan G. Peeke, A. D. Seroczynski, Jane M. Tram, K. B. Hoffman, M. D. Ruiz, Farrah Jacquez, and Tracy Maschman. 2001. "The Development of Multiple Domains of Child and Adolescent Self-Concept: A Cohort Sequential Longitudinal Design." *Child Development* 72 (6): 1723–46.

Costello, E. Jane, Debra L. Foley, and Adrian Angold. 2006. "10-Year Research Update Review: The Epidemiology of Child and Adolescent Psychiatric Disorders: II. Developmental Epidemiology"." *Journal of the American Academy of Child and Adolescent Psychiatry* 45: 8–25.

Costello, E. Jane, Sarah Mustillo, Alaattin Erkanli, Gordon Keeler, and Adrian Angold. 2003. "Prevalence and Development of Psychiatric Disorders in Childhood and Adolescence." *Archives of General Psychiatry* 60 (8): 837–44. doi:10.1001/archpsyc.60.8.837.

Coyne, James C. 1976a. "Toward an Interactional Description of Depression". *Psychiatry* 39 (1): 28.

Coyne, James C. 1976b. "Depression and the Response of Others." *Journal of Abnormal Psychology* 85 (2): 186–93. doi:10.1037/0021-843X.93.4.477.

Curry, John, Paul Rohde, Anne Simons, Susan Silva, Benedetto Vitiello, Christopher Kratochvil, Mark Reinecke, et al. 2006. "Predictors and Moderators of Acute Outcome in the Treatment for Adolescents with Depression Study

(TADS)." *Journal of the American Academy of Child and Adolescent Psychiatry* 45 (12): 1427–39. doi:10.1097/01.chi.0000240838.78984.e2.

Curtin, Sally C., Margaret Warner, and Holly Hedegaard. 2016. "Increase in Suicide in the United States, 1999–2014" (NCHS Data Brief no. 241). Hyattsville, MD: National Center for Health Statistics. www.cdc.gov/nchs/products/databriefs/db241.htm.

David-Ferdon, Corrine, and Nadine J. Kaslow. 2008. "Evidence-Based Psychosocial Treatments for Child and Adolescent Depression." *Journal of Clinical Child & Adolescent Psychology* 37: 62–104. doi:10.1080/15374410701817865.

Dawes, Robyn M., David Faust, and Paul E. Meehl. 1989. "Clinical Versus Actuarial Judgment." *Science* 243 (4899): 1668–74.

Dougherty, Lea R., Daniel N. Klein, Thomas M. Olino, and Rebecca S. Laptook. 2008. "Depression in Children and Adolescents." In *A Guide to Assessments That Work*, edited by John Hunsley and Eric K. Mash, 69–95. New York, NY: Oxford University Press. doi:10.1093/med:psych/9780195310641.003.0004.

Dowdney, Linda. 2000. "Annotation: Childhood Bereavement Following Parental Death." *The Journal of Child Psychology and Psychiatry* 41 (7): 819–30. doi:10.1111/1469-7610.00670.

Dunn, Valerie, and Ian M. Goodyer. 2006. "Longitudinal Investigation Into Childhood- and Adolescence-onset Depression: Psychiatric Outcome in Early Adulthood." *The British Journal of Psychiatry* 188 (3): 216–22. doi:10.1192/bjp.188.3.216.

Durbin, C. Emily, and Sylia Wilson. 2009. "Assessment of Mood Disorders in Children and Adolescents." In *Assessing Childhood Psychopathology and Developmental Disabilities*, edited by Johnny L. Matson, Frank Andrasik, and Michael L. Matson, 241–71. New York, NY: Springer Science + Business Media. doi:10.1007/978-0-387-09528-8_9.

Eaton, William W., Corey Smith, Michele Ybarra, Carles Muntaner, and Allen Tien. 2004. "Center for Epidemiologic Studies Depression Scale: Review and Revision (CESD and CESD-R)." In *The Use of Psychological Testing for Treatment Planning and Outcomes Assessment: Volume 3: Instruments for Adults*, 3rd ed., edited by Mark E. Maruish, 363–77. Mahwah, NJ: Lawrence Erlbaum Associates Publishers.

Emslie, Graham J, Daniel Ventura, Andrew Korotzer, and Stavros Tourkodimitris. 2009. "Escitalopram in the Treatment of Adolescent Depression: A Randomized Placebo-Controlled Multisite Trial." *Journal of the American Academy of Child and Adolescent Psychiatry* 48 (7): 721–9. doi:10.1097/CHI.0b013e3181a2b304.

Feldman, Mitchell D., Peter Franks, Paul R. Duberstein, Steven Vannoy, Ronald Epstein, and Richard L. Kravitz. 2007. "Let's Not Talk About it: Suicide Inquiry in Primary Care." *Annals of Family Medicine* 5 (5): 412–8. doi:10.1370/afm.719.

Findling, Robert L., Adelaide Robb, and Anjana Bose. 2013. "Escitalopram in the Treatment of Adolescent Depression: A Randomized, Double-Blind, Placebo-Controlled Extension Trial." *Journal of Child and Adolescent Psychopharmacology* 23 (7): 468–80. doi:10.1089/cap.2012.0023.

Garber, Judy, and Cynthia Flynn. 2001. "Predictors of Depressive Cognitions in Young Adolescents." *Cognitive Therapy and Research* 25 (4): 353–76. doi:10.1023/A:1005530402239.

Garland, Ann F., Marc Kruse, and Gregory A. Aarons. 2003. "Clinicians and Outcome Measurement: What's the Use?" *The Journal of Behavioral Health Services & Research* 30 (4): 393–405. doi:10.1007/BF02287427.

Ge, Xiaojia, Rand D. Conger, and Glen H. Elder and Jr. 1996. "Coming of Age Too Early : Pubertal Influences on Girls' Vulnerability to Psychological Distress." *Child Development* 67 (6): 3386–400.

Giedd, Jay N. 2008. "The Teen Brain: Insights from Neuroimaging." *Journal of Adolescent Health* 42 (4): 335–43.

Giletta, Matteo, Ron H. J. Scholte, William J. Burk, Rutger C. M. E. Engels, Junilla K. Larsen, Mitchell J. Prinstein, and Silvia Ciairano. 2011. "Similarity in Depressive Symptoms in Adolescents' Friendship Dyads: Selection or Socialization?" *Developmental Psychology* 47 (6): 1804–14. doi:10.1037/a0023872.

Goodyer, Ian M., Joe Herbert, Sandra M. Secher, and Josephine Pearson. 1997. "Short-Term Outcome of Major Depression: I. Comorbidity and Severity at Presentation as Predictors of Persistent Disorder." *Journal of the American Academy of Child & Adolescent Psychiatry* 36 (2): 179–87. doi:10.1097/00004583-199702000-00008.

Goodyer, Ian M., Rebecca J. Park, and Joe Herbert. 2001a. "Psychosocial and Endocrine Features of Chronic First-Episode Major Depression in 8–16 Year Olds." *Biological Psychiatry* 50 (5): 351–7. doi:10.1016/S0006-3223(01)01120-9.

Goodyer, Ian M., Rebecca J. Park, Clare M. Netherton, and Joe Herbert. 2001b. "Possible Role of Cortisol and Dehydroepiadrosterone in Human Development and Psychopathology." *British Journal of Psychiatry* 179: 243–49. doi:10.1192/bjp.179.3.243.

Gould, Madelyn S., Robert King, Steven Greenwald, Prudence Fisher, Mary Schwab-Stone, Rachel Kramer, Alan J. Flisher, Sherryl Goodman, Glorisa Canino, and David Shaffer. 1998. "Psychopathology Associated with Suicidal Ideation and Attempts Among Children and Adolescents." *Journal of the American Academy of Child & Adolescent Psychiatry* 37 (9): 915–23.

Gould, Madelyn S., Frank A. Marrocco, Marjorie Kleinman, John Graham Thomas, Katherine Mostkoff, Jean Cote, and Mark Davies. 2005. "Evaluating Iatrogenic Risk of Youth Suicide Screening Programs: A Randomized

Controlled Trial." *Journal of the American Medical Association,* 293 (13): 1635–43. doi:10.1001/jama.293.13.1635.

Graber, Julia A., Peter M. Lewinsohn, John R. Seeley, and Jeanne Brooks-Gunn. 1997. "Is Psychopathology Associated With the Timing of Pubertal Development?" The Journal of the American Academy of Child and Adolescent Psychiatry: 36 (12): 1768–76. doi:10.1097/00004583-199712000-00026.

Hamilton, Jessica L., Jonathan P. Stange, Lyn Y. Abramson, and Lauren B. Alloy. 2015. "Stress and the Development of Cognitive Vulnerabilities to Depression Explain Sex Differences in Depressive Symptoms during Adolescence." *Clinical Psychological Science* 3 (5): 702–14. doi:10.1177/2167702614545479.

Hammad, Tarek A., Thomas P. Laughren, and Judith A. Racoosin. 2006. "Suicide Rates in Short-term Randomized Controlled Trials of Newer Antidepressants." *Journal of Clinical Psychopharmacology* 26 (2): 203–7.

Hammen, Constance L. 1991. *Depression Runs in Families: The Social Context of Risk and Resilience in Children of Depressed Mothers.* New York, NY: Springer-Verlag.

Hankin, Benjamin L. 2009. "Development of Sex Differences in Depressive and Co-Occurring Anxious Symptoms during Adolescence: Descriptive Trajectories and Potential Explanations in a Multiwave Prospective Study." *Journal of Clinical Child & Adolescent Psychology* 38 (4): 460–72. doi:10.1080/15374410902976288.

Hankin, Benjamin L., Lyn Y. Abramson, Terrie E. Moffitt, Phil A. Silva, Rob McGee, and Kathryn E. Angell. 1998. "Development of Depression from Preadolescence to Young Adulthood: Emerging Gender Differences in a 10-Year Longitudinal Study." *Journal of Abnormal Psychology* 107: 128–40. doi:10.1037/0021-843X.107.1.128.

Hartup, Willard W. 1996. "The Company They Keep: Friendships and Their Developmental Significance." *Child Development* 67 (1): 1–13.

Hawker, David S. J., and Michael J. Boulton. 2000. "Twenty Years' Research on Peer Victimization and Psychosocial Maladjustment: A Meta-Analytic Review of Cross-Sectional Studies." *Journal of Child Psychology and Psychiatry, and Allied Disciplines* 41 (4): 441–55. doi:10.1111/1469-7610.00629.

Hodges, Ernest V. E., and David G. Perry. 1999. "Personal and Interpersonal Antecedents and Consequences of Victimization by Peers." *Journal of Personality and Social Psychology* 76 (4): 677–85.

Hoffman, Kit B, David A. Cole, Joan M. Martin, Jane Tram, and A. D. Seroczynski. 2000. "Are the Discrepancies between Self- and Others' Appraisals of Competence Predictive or Reflective of Depressive Symptoms in Children and Adolescents: A Longitudinal Study, Part II." *Journal of Abnormal Psychology* 109 (4): 651–62. doi:10.1037/0021-843X.109.4.651.

Hughes, Carrol W., Graham J. Emslie, M. Lynn Crismon, Kelly Posner, Boris Birmaher, Neal Ryan, Peter Jensen, et al. 2007. "Texas Children's Medication

Algorithm Project: Update From Texas Consensus Conference Panel on Medication Treatment of Childhood Major Depressive Disorder." *Journal of the American Academy of Child & Adolescent Psychiatry 46* (6), 667–86.

Hunsley, John, and Eric J. Mash. 2010. "The Role of Assessment in Evidence-Based Practice." In *Handbook of Assessment and Treatment Planning for Psychological Disorders*, 2nd ed., edited by Martin M. Antony, David H. Barlow, 3–22. New York, NY: Guilford Press.

Hyde, Janet Shibley, Amy H. Mezulis, and Lyn Y. Abramson. 2008. "The ABCs of Depression: Integrating Affective, Biological, and Cognitive Models to Explain the Emergence of the Gender Difference in Depression." *Psychological Review* 115 (2): 291–313. doi:10.1037/0033-295X.115.2.291.

Jacobson, Colleen M., and Laura Mufson. 2010. "Treating Adolescent Depression Using Interpersonal Psychotherapy." In *Evidence-Based Psychotherapies for Children and Adolescents*, edited by John R. Weisz and Alan E. Kazdin, 140–55. New York, NY: Guilford Press.

Jeffreys, Megan, and W. Robin Weersing. 2014. "Depressive Disorders in Adolescents." In *Comprehensive Evidence Based Interventions for Children and Adolescents*, edited by Candice A. Alfano and Deborah C. Beidel, 147–61. Hoboken, NJ: John Wiley & Sons Inc.

Jensen, Peter S., Maritza Rubio-Stipec, Glorisa Canino, Hector R. Bird, Mina K. Dulcan, Mary E. Schwab-Stone, and Benjamin B. Lahey. 1999. "Parent and Child Contributions to Diagnosis of Mental Disorder: Are Both Informants Always Necessary?" *Journal of the American Academy of Child & Adolescent Psychiatry* 38 (12): 1569–79. doi:10.1097/00004583-199912000-00019.

Joiner, Thomas E. 1994. "Contagious Depression: Existence, Specificity to Depressed Symptoms, and the Role of Reassurance Seeking." *Journal of Personality and Social Psychology* 67 (2): 287–96. doi:10.1037/0022-3514.67.2.287.

Joiner, Thomas E., Mark S. Alfano, and Gerald I. Metalsky. 1992. "When Depression Breeds Contempt: Reassurance Seeking, Self-Esteem, and Rejection of Depressed College Students by Their Roommates." *Journal of Abnormal Psychology* 101 (1): 165–73. doi:10.1037/0021-843X.101.1.165.

Joiner, Thomas E., and Jeffrey Barnett. 1994. "A Test of Interpersonal Theory of Depression in Children and Adolescents Using a Projective Technique." *Journal of Abnormal Child Psychology* 22 (5): 595.

Joiner, Thomas E., Gerald I. Metalsky, Jennifer Katz, and Steven R. H. Beach. 1999. "Depression and Excessive Reassurance-Seeking." *Psychological Inquiry* 10 (3): 269–78. doi:10.1207/S15327965PLI1004_1.

Kaltiala-Heino, Riittakerttu, Elise Kosunen, and Matti Rimpela. 2003. "Pubertal Timing, Sexual Behaviour and Self-Reported Depression in Middle Adolescence." *Journal of Adolescence* 26 (5): 531–45. doi:10.1016/S0140-1971(03)00053-8.

Kamper, Kimberly E., and Jamie M. Ostrov. 2013. "Relational Aggression in Middle Childhood Predicting Adolescent Social-Psychological Adjustment: The Role of Friendship Quality." *Journal of Clinical Child and Adolescent Psychology* 42 (6): 855.

Kaslow, Nadine J., Marissa N. Petersen-Coleman, and Ashley Maehr Alexander. 2014. "Biological and Psychosocial Interventions for Depression in Children and Adolescents." In *Handbook of Depression*, 3rd ed., edited by Ian H. Gotlib and Constance L. Hammen, 571–89. New York, NY: Guilford Press.

Kaslow, Nadine J., Kevin D. Stark, Brian Printz, Ronnie Livingston, and Shung Ling Tsai. 1992. "Cognitive Triad Inventory for Children: Development and Relation to Depression and Anxiety." *Journal of Clinical Child Psychology*. doi:10.1207/s15374424jccp2104_3.

Kaufman, Joan, Boris Birmaher, David Brenr, Uma Rao, Cynthia Flynn, Paula Moreci, Douglas Williamson, and Neal Ryan. 1997. "Schedule for Affective Disorders and Schizophrenia for School-Age Children-Present and Lifetime Version (K-SADS-PL): Initial Reliability and Validity Data." *Journal of the American Academy of Child & Adolescent Psychiatry* 36 (7): 980–8. doi:10.1097/00004583-199707000-00021.

Kendall, Philip C., Dennis P. Cantwell, and Alan E. Kazdin. 1989. "Depression in Children and Adolescents: Assessment Issues and Recommendations." *Cognitive Therapy And Research* 13, 109–46. doi:10.1007/BF01173268.

Kennard, Betsy D., Graham J. Emslie, Taryn L. Mayes, and Jennifer L. Hughes. 2006. "Relapse and Recurrence in Pediatric Depression." *Child and Adolescent Psychiatric Clinics of North America* 15 (4): 1057–79. doi:10.1016/j.chc.2006.05.003.

Kennard, Betsy D., Graham J. Emslie, Taryn L. Mayes, Paul A. Nakonezny, Jessica M. Jones, Aleksandra A. Foxwell, and Jessica King. 2014. "Sequential Treatment with Fluoxetine and Relapse-Prevention CBT to Improve Outcomes in Pediatric Depression." *American Journal of Psychiatry* 171 (10): 1083–90. doi:10.1176/appi.ajp.2014.13111460.

Kingery, Julie Newman, Cynthia A. Erdley, and Katherine C. Marshall. 2011. "Peer Acceptance and Friendship as Predictors of Early Adolescents' Adjustment across the Middle School Transition." *Merrill-Palmer Quarterly* 57 (3): 215–43.

Kirsch, Irving. 2014. "Antidepressants and the Placebo Effect"." *Zeitschrift für Psychologie* 222 (3): 128–34. doi:10.1027/2151-2604/a000176.

Klein, Daniel N., Lea R. Dougherty, and Thomas M. Olino. 2005. "Toward Guidelines for Evidence-Based Assessment of Depression in Children and Adolescents." *Journal of Clinical Child & Adolescent Psychology* 34 (3): 412–32. doi:10.1207/s15374424jccp3403_3.

Klein, Daniel N., Paige C. Ouimette, Helen S. Kelly, Tova Ferro, and Lawrence P. Riso. 1994. "Test-Retest Reliability of Team Consensus Best-Estimate Diagnoses of Axis I and II Disorders in a Family Study." *The American Journal of Psychiatry* 151 (7): 1043.

Klomek, Anat Brunstein, and Laura Mufson. 2006. "Interpersonal Psychotherapy for Depressed Adolescents." *Child and Adolescent Psychiatric Clinics of North America* 15 (4): 959–75. doi:10.1016/j.chc.2006.05.005.

Kovacs, M. 2010. *Children's Depression Inventory.* 2nd ed. North Tonawanda, NY: Multi-Health System.

La Greca, Annette M., and Hannah Moore Harrison. 2005. "Adolescent Peer Relations, Friendships, and Romantic Relationships: Do They Predict Social Anxiety and Depression?" *Journal of Clinical Child & Adolescent Psychology* 34 (1): 49–61.

La Greca, Annette M., Betty S. Lai, Maria M. Llabre, Wendy K. Silverman, Eric M. Vernberg, and Mitchell J. Prinstein. 2013. "Children's Postdisaster Trajectories of PTS Symptoms: Predicting Chronic Distress." *Child and Youth Care Forum* 42 (4): 351–69. doi:10.1007/s10566-013-9206-1.

Lakdawalla, Zia, Benjamin L. Hankin, and Robin Mermelstein. 2007. "Cognitive Theories of Depression in Children and Adolescents: A Conceptual and Quantitative Review." *Clinical Child and Family Psychology Review* 10: 1–24. doi:10.1007/s10567-006-0013-1.

Lambert, Michael J., Nathan B. Hansen, and Arthur E. Finch. 2001. "Patient-Focused Research: Using Patient Outcome Data to Enhance Treatment Effects." *Journal of Consulting and Clinical Psychology* 69 (2): 159–72. doi:10.1037/0022-006X.69.2.159.

Lansford, Jennifer E., Patrick S. Malone, Domini R. Castellino, Kenneth A. Dodge, Gregory S. Pettit, and John E. Bates. 2006. "Trajectories of Internalizing, Externalizing, and Grades for Children Who Have and Have Not Experienced Their Parents' Divorce or Separation." *Journal of Family Psychology* 20 (2): 292–301. doi:10.1037/0893-3200.20.2.292.

Lawrence, Margaret T., and John R. Ureda. 1990. "Student Recognition of and Response to Suicidal Peers." *Suicide & Life-Threatening Behavior* 20 (2): 164.

Leventhal, Allan M., and David O. Antonuccio. 2009. "On Chemical Imbalances, Antidepressants, and the Diagnosis of Depression." *Ethical Human Psychology and Psychiatry* 11 (3): 199–214.

Lewinsohn, P. M. 1974. "A Behavioral Approach to Depression." In *The Psychology of Depression: Contemporary Theory and Research,* edited by Raymond J. Friedman and Martin M. Katz, 157–78. New York, NY: John Wiley & Sons.

Lewinsohn, Peter M., Gregory N. Clarke, Hyman Hops, and Judy Andrews. 1990. "Cognitive-Behavioral Treatment for Depressed Adolescents." *Behavior Therapy* 21 (4): 385–401. doi:10.1016/S0005-7894(05)80353-3.

Lewinsohn, Peter M., Gregory N. Clarke, John R. Seeley, and Paul Rohde. 1994. "Major Depression in Community Adolescents: Age at Onset, Episode Duration, and Time to Recurrence." *Journal of the American Academy of Child and Adolescent Psychiatry* 33 (6): 809–18. doi:10.1097/00004583-199407000-00006.

Lewinsohn, Peter M., Paul Rohde, John R. Seeley, Daniel N. Klein, and Ian H. Gotlib. 2000. "Natural Course of Adolescent Major Depressive Disorder in a Community Sample: Predictors of Recurrence in Young Adults." *The American Journal of Psychiatry* 157 (10): 1584–91. doi:10.1176/appi.ajp.157.10.1584.

Little, Stephanie A., and Judy Garber. 2005. "The Role of Social Stressors and Interpersonal Orientation in Explaining the Longitudinal Relation between Externalizing and Depressive Symptoms." *Journal of Abnormal Psychology* 114 (3): 432–43. doi:10.1037/0021-843x.114.3.432.

Lloyd, Camille. 1980. "Life Events and Depressive Disorder Reviewed: I. Events as Predisposing Factors." *Archives of General Psychiatry* 37 (5): 529–35. doi:10.1001/archpsyc.1980.01780180043004.

Lonigan, Christopher J., Jean C. Elbert and Suzanne Bennett. 1998. "Empirically Supported Psychosocial Interventions for Children: An Overview." *Journal of Clinical Child Psychology* 27 (2): 138–45.

March, John, Susan Silva, Stephen Petrycki, John Curry, Karen Wells, John Fairbank, Barbara Burns, et al. 2004. "Fluoxetine, Cognitive-Behavioral Therapy, and their Combination for Adolescents with Depression: Treatment for Adolescents with Depression Study (TADS) Randomized Controlled Trial." *Journal of the American Medical Association* 292 (7): 807–20.

March, John S., Susan Silva, Stephen Petrycki, John Curry, Karen Wells, John Fairbank, Barbara Burns, et al. 2007. "The Treatment for Adolescents with Depression Study (TADS): Long-term Effectiveness and Safety Outcomes." *Archives of General Psychiatry* 64 (10): 1132.

Mark, Tami L., Katherine R. Levit, and Jeffrey A. Buck. 2009. "Psychotropic Drug Prescriptions by Medical Speciality." *Psychiatric Services* 60 (9): 1167. doi:10.1176/appi.ps.60.9.1167.

Mash, Eric J., and John Hunsley. 2005. "Evidence-Based Assessment of Child and Adolescent Disorders: Issues and Challenges." *Journal of Clinical Child & Adolescent Psychology* 34 (3): 362–79. doi:10.1207/s15374424jccp3403_1.

McCauley, Elizabeth, Jeffrey R. Mitchell, Patrick Burke, and Sheila Moss. 1988. "Cognitive Attributes of Depression in Children and Adolescents." *Journal of Consulting and Clinical Psychology* 56 (6): 903–8. doi:10.1037/0022-006X.56.6.903.

McDougall, Patricia, and Shelley Hymel. 2007. "Same-Gender Versus Cross-Gender Friendship Conceptions: Similar or Different?" *Merrill-Palmer Quarterly* 53 (3): 347–80.

Merikangas, Kathleen Ries, Jian-ping He, Marcy Burstein, Joel Swendsen, Shelli Avenevoli, Brady Case, Katholiki Georgiades, et al. 2011. "Service Utilization for Lifetime Mental Disorders in U.S. Adolescents: Results of the National Comorbidity Survey-Adolescent Supplement (NCS-A)." *Journal of the American Academy of Child and Adolescent Psychiatry* 50: 32–45. doi:10.1016/j.jaac.2010.10.006.

Merikangas, Kathleen Ries, Erin F. Nakamura, and Ronald C. Kessler. 2009. "Epidemiology of Mental Disorders in Children and Adolescents." *Dialogues in Clinical Neuroscience* 11: 7–20.

Michl, Louisa C., Katie A. McLaughlin, Kathrine Shepherd, and Susan Nolen-Hoeksema. 2013. "Rumination as a Mechanism Linking Stressful Life Events to Symptoms of Depression and Anxiety: Longitudinal Evidence in Early Adolescents and Adults." *Journal of Abnormal Psychology* 122 (2): 339–52. doi:10.1037/a0031994.

Mufson, Laura H., Kristen Pollack Dorta, Donna Moreau, and Myrna M. Weissman. 2004. *Interpersonal Psychotherapy for Depressed Adolescents.* 2nd ed. New York, NY: The Guilford Press.

Mufson, Laura, and Rebecca Sills. 2006. "Interpersonal Psychotherapy for Depressed Adolescents (IPT-A): An Overview." *Nordic Journal of Psychiatry* 60 (6): 431–7. doi:10.1080/08039480601022397.

Mufson, Laura, Myrna M. Weissman, Donna Moreau, and Robin Garfinkel. 1999. "Efficacy of Interpersonal Psychotherapy for Depressed Adolescents." *Archives of General Psychiatry* 56 (6): 573–9. doi:10.1001/archpsyc.56 .6.573.

Murphy, George E. 1975. "The Physician's Responsibility for Suicide. I. An Error of Commission." *Annals of Internal Medicine, 82,* 301–4. doi:10.7326/0003-4819-82-3-301.

Nagar, Saurabh, Jeffrey T. Sherer, Hua Chen, and Rajender R. Aparasu. 2010. "Extent of Functional Impairment in Children and Adolescents with Depression." *Current Medical Research and Opinion* 26 (9): 2057–64. doi:10.1185/03007995.2010.496688.

National Institute for Health and Clinical Excellence (NICE). 2013. "Depression in Children and Young People: Quality Standard." https://www.nice.org.uk/guidance/qs48.

Naughton, Marie, Jane B. Mulrooney, and Brian E. Leonard. 2000. "A Review of the Role of Serotonin Receptors in Psychiatric Disorders." *Human Psychopharmacology: Clinical and Experimental* 15 (6): 397–415.

Nolen-Hoeksema, Susan. 2001. "Gender Differences in Depression." *Current Directions in Psychological Science* 10 (5): 173–6. doi:10.1111/1467-8721.00142.

Nolen-Hoeksema, Susan. 1991. "Responses to Depression and Their Effects on the Duration of Depressive Episodes." *Journal of Abnormal Psychology* 100 (4): 569–82. doi:10.1037/0021-843X.100.4.569.

Olfson, Mark, Carlos Blanco, Shuai Wang, Gonzalo Laje, and Christoph U. Correll. 2013. "National Trends in the Mental Health Care of Children, Adolescents, and Adults by Office-Based Physicians." *JAMA Psychiatry* 71: 81–90. doi:10.1001/jamapsychiatry.2013.3074.

Olfson, Mark, Marc J. Gameroff, Steven C. Marcus, and Bruce D. Waslick. 2003. "Outpatient Treatment of Child and Adolescent Depression in the United States." *Archives of General Psychiatry* 60 (12): 1236–42.

Olfson, Mark, and Steven C. Marcus. 2010. "National Trends in Outpatient Psychotherapy." *American Journal of Psychiatry* 167 (12): 1456–63. doi:10.1176/appi.ajp.2010.10040570.

Oppenheimer, Caroline W., and Benjamin L. Hankin. 2011. "Relationship Quality and Depressive Symptoms Among Adolescents: A Short-Term Multiwave Investigation of Longitudinal, Reciprocal Associations." *Journal of Clinical Child & Adolescent Psychology* 40 (3): 486–93. doi:10.1080/15374 416.2011.563462.

Orvaschel, Helen. 2004. "Depressive Disorders." In *Psychological Assessment in Clinical Practice: A Pragmatic Guide*, edited by Michel Hersen, 297–319. New York, NY: Brunner-Routledge.

Parker, Jeffrey G., and Steven R. Asher. 1987. "Peer Relations and Later Personal Adjustment: Are Low-Accepted Children at Risk?" *Psychological Bulletin* 102 (3): 357–89. doi:10.1037/0033-2909.102.3.357.

Pine, Daniel S., Elizabeth Cohen, Patricia Cohen, and Judith Brook. 1999. "Adolescent Depressive Symptoms as Predictors of Adult Depression: Moodiness or Mood Disorder?" *The American Journal of Psychiatry* 156: 133–5. doi:10.1176/ajp.156.1.133.

Poletti, Michele. 2009. "Adolescent Brain Development and Executive Functions: A Prefrontal Framework for Developmental Psychopathologies." *Clinical Neuropsychiatry* 6 (4): 155–65.

Pomerantz, Eva M. 2001. "Parent × Child Socialization: Implications for the Development of Depressive Symptoms." *Journal of Family Psychology* 15 (3): 510–25.

Poznanski, Elva O., Linda.N. Freeman, and Hartmut B. Mokros. 1985. "Children's Depression Rating Scale Revised." *Psychopharmacology Bulletin* 21: 979–89.

Preddy, Teresa M., and Paula J. Fite. 2012. "The Impact of Aggression Subtypes and Friendship Quality on Child Symptoms of Depression." *Child Indicators Research* 5 (4): 705–18. doi:10.1007/s12187-012-9143-9.

Prinstein, Mitchell J. 2007. "Moderators of Peer Contagion: A Longitudinal Examination of Depression Socialization between Adolescents and Their Best

Friends." *Journal of Clinical Child & Adolescent Psychology* 36 (2): 159–70. doi:10.1080/15374410701274934.

Prinstein, Mitchell J., and Julie Wargo Aikins. 2004. "Cognitive Moderators of the Longitudinal Association between Peer Rejection and Adolescent Depressive Symptoms." *Journal of Abnormal Child Psychology* 32 (2): 147–58. doi:10.1023/B:JACP.0000019767.55592.63.

Prinstein, Mitchell J., Julie Boergers, and Anthony Spirito. 2001. "Adolescents' and Their Friends' Health-Risk Behavior: Factors that Alter or Add to Peer Influence." *Journal of Pediatric Psychology* 26 (5): 287–98. doi:10.1093/jpepsy/26.5.287.

Prinstein, Mitchell J., Julie Boergers, and Eric M. Vernberg. 2001. "Overt and Relational Aggression in Adolescents: Social-Psychological Adjustment of Aggressors and Victims." *Journal of Clinical Child Psychology* 30 (4): 479.

Prinstein, Mitchell J., Jessica L. Borelli, Charissa S. L. Cheah, Valerie A. Simon, and Julie Wargo Aikins. 2005. "Adolescent Girls' Interpersonal Vulnerability to Depressive Symptoms: A Longitudinal Examination of Reassurance Seeking and Peer Relationships." *Journal of Abnormal Psychology* 114 (4): 676–88. doi:10.1037/0021-843x.114.4.676.

Quiggle, Nancy L., Judy Garber, William F Panak, and Kenneth A. Dodge. 1992. "Social Information Processing in Aggressive and Depressed Children." *Child Development* 63 (6): 1305–20.

Reynolds, W. M. 2002. *RCDS-2 (Reynolds Child Depression Scale-2nd edition) Professional Manual*. Edited by Psychological Assessment Resources. Lutz, FL: Psychological Assessment Resources.

Reynolds, William M. 2004. "Reynolds Adolescent Depression Scale—2nd Edition." In *Comprehensive Handbook of Psychological Assessment, Volume 2: Personality Assessment*, edited by Mark J. Hilsenroth, Daniel L. Segal, and Michel Hersen, 224–36. New York, NY: John Wiley & Sons.

Rhoades, Kimberly A. 2008. "Children's Responses to Interparental Conflict : A Meta-Analysis of Their Associations with Child Adjustment." *Child Development* 79 (6): 1942–56.

Rice, Frances, Gordon Harold, and Anita Thapar. 2002. "The Aetiology of Childhood Depression: A Review of Genetic Influences." *Journal of Child Psychology and Psychiatry* 43 (1): 65–79. doi:10.1111/1469-7610.00004.

Roberts, Robert E., C. Clifford Attkisson, and Abram Rosenblatt. 1998. "Prevalence of Psychopathology among Children and Adolescents." *The American Journal of Psychiatry* 155 (6): 715–25.

Roeser, Robert W., Jacquelynne S. Eccles, and Karen R. Strobel. 1998. "Linking the Study of Schooling and Mental Health: Selected Issues and Empirical Illustrations at the Level of the Individual." *Educational Psychologist* 33 (4): 153–76. doi:10.1207/s15326985ep3304_2.

Rohr, Uwe D. 2002. "The Impact of Testosterone Imbalance on Depression and Women's Health." *Maturitas* 41 Suppl 1: S25–S46. doi:10.1016/S0378-5122(02)00013-0.

Rose, Amanda J. 2002. "Co-rumination in the Friendships of Girls and Boys." *Child Development* 73 (6): 1830–43.

Rose, Amanda J., Wendy Carlson, and Erika M. Waller. 2007. "Prospective Associations of Co-Rumination with Friendship and Emotional Adjustment: Considering the Socioemotional Trade-Offs of Co-Rumination." *Developmental Psychology* 43 (4): 1019–31. doi:10.1037/0012-1649.43.4.1019.

Rudolph, Karen D., and Constance Hammen. 1999. "Age and Gender as Determinants of Stress Exposure, Generation, and Reactions in Youngsters: A transactional Perspective." *Child Development* 70 (3): 660–77.

Rudolph, Karen D., Gary Ladd, and Lisa Dinella. 2007. "Gender Differences in the Interpersonal Consequences of Early-Onset Depressive Symptoms." *Merrill-Palmer Quarterly* 53 (3): 461–88.

Rutter, Michael. 2006. *Genes and Behavior: Nature—Nurture Interplay Explained.* Malden, MA: Wiley-Blackwell.

Rutter, Michael, Terrie E. Moffitt, and Avshalom Caspi. 2006. "Gene-Environment Interplay and Psychopathology: Multiple Varieties but Real Effects." *Journal of Child Psychology and Psychiatry and Allied Disciplines* 47 (3–4): 226–61. doi:10.1111/j.1469-7610.2005.01557.x

Santor, Darcy A., Michelle Gregus, and Andrew Welch. 2006. "Eight Decades of Measurement in Depression." *Measurement: Interdisciplinary Research and Perspectives* 4 (3): 135–55. doi:10.1207/s15366359mea0403_1.

Schwartz-Mette, Rebecca A., and Amanda J. Rose. 2009. "Conversational Self-Focus in Adolescent Friendships: Observational Assessment of an Interpersonal Process and Relations with Internalizing Symptoms and Friendship Quality." *Journal of Social and Clinical Psychology* 28 (10): 1263–97. doi:10.1521/jscp.2009.28.10.1263.

Schwartz-Mette, Rebecca A., and Amanda J. Rose. 2012. "Co-Rumination Mediates Contagion of Internalizing Symptoms within Youths' Friendships." *Developmental Psychology* 48 (5): 1355–65. doi:10.1037/a0027484.

Schwartz-Mette, Rebecca A., and Amanda J. Rose. 2016. "Depressive Symptoms and Conversational Self-focus in Adolescents' Friendships." *Journal of Abnormal Child Psychology* 44: 87–100.

Schwartz-Mette, Rebecca A., and Rhiannon Smith. In press. "When Does Co-Rumination Facilitate Depression Contagion in Adolescent Friendships? Investigating Intrapersonal and Interpersonal Factors." *Journal of Clinical Child and Adolescent Psychology.* doi: 10.1080/15374416.2016.1197837.

Seedat, Soraya. 2014. "Controversies in the Use of Antidepressants in Children and Adolescents: A Decade since the Storm and Where Do We Stand Now?" *Journal of Child and Adolescent Mental Health* 26 (2): iii-v.

Seligman, Martin E. P., Karen Reivich, Lisa Jaycox, and Jane Gillham. 1995. *The Optimistic Child*. Boston, MA: Houghton Mifflin.

Shaffer, David, Prudence Fisher, Christopher P. Lucas, Mina K. Dulcan, and Mary E. Schwab-Stone. 2000. "NIMH Diagnostic Interview Schedule for Children, Version IV (NIMH DISC-IV): Description, Differences from Previous Versions, and Reliability of Some Common Diagnoses." *Journal of the American Academy of Child and Adolescent Psychiatry* 39, 28–38.

Shalev, Idan, Elad Lerer, Salomon Israel, Florina Uzefovsky, Inga Gritsenko, David Mankuta, Richard P. Ebstein, and Marsha Kaitz. 2009. "BDNF Val66Met Polymorphism Is Associated with HPA Axis Reactivity to Psychological Stress Characterized by Genotype and Gender Interactions." *Psychoneuroendocrinology* 34 (3): 382–88. doi:10.1016/j.psyneuen.2008.09.017.

Shores, Molly M, and Alvin M Matsumoto. 2014. "Testosterone, Aging and Survival: Biomarker or Deficiency." *Current Opinion in Endocrinology, Diabetes, and Obesity* 21 (3): 209–16. doi:10.1097/MED.0000000000000057.

Sohrabji, Farida, and Danielle K. Lewis. 2006. "Estrogen—BDNF Interactions: Implications for Neurodegenerative Diseases." *Neuroendocrinology* 27 (4): 404–14. doi:10.1016/j.yfrne.2006.09.003.

Sowislo, Julia Friederike, and Ulrich Orth. 2013. "Does Low Self-Esteem Predict Depression and Anxiety? A Meta-Analysis of Longitudinal Studies." *Psychological Bulletin* 139 (1): 213–40. doi:10.1037/a0028931.

Stark, Kevin D., William M. Reynolds, and Nadine J. Kaslow. 1987. "A Comparison of the Relative Efficacy of Self-Control Therapy and a Behavioral Problem-Solving Therapy for Depression in Children." *Journal of Abnormal Child Psychology* 15: 91–113.

Stark, Kevin D., Lawrence W. Rouse, and Ronald Livingston. 1991. "Treatment of Depression during Childhood and Adolescence: Cognitive-Behavioral Procedures for the Individual and Family" In *Child and Adolescent Therapy: Cognitive-Behavioral Procedures*, edited by Philip C. Kendall, 165–98. New York, NY: Guilford Press.

Stark, Kevin D., Janay Sander, Michelle Hauser, Jane Simpson, Sarah Schnoebelen, Rand Glenn, and Johanna Molnar. 2006. "Depressive Disorders During Childhood and Adolescence." In *Treatment of Childhood Disorders*, 3rd ed., edited by Eric J. Mash and Russel A. Barkley, 336–407. New York, NY: Guilford Press.

Stark, Kevin D., Sarah Schnoebelen, Jennifer Hargrave, Johanna Molnar, and Rand Glen. 2011. *'ACTION' Workbook: Cognitive-Behavioral Therapy for Treating Depressed Boys*. Ardmore, PA: Workbook Publishing.

Stark, Kevin D., Sarah Schnoebelen, Jane Simpson, Jennifer Hargrave, Johanna Molnar, and Rand Glen. 2007. *Treating Depressed Youth: Therapist Manual for 'ACTION'*. Ardmore, PA: Workbook Publishing.

Stark, Kevin D., William Streusand, Prerna Arora, and Puja Patel. 2011. "Childhood Depression: The ACTION Treatment Program." In *Child and*

*Adolescent Therapy: Cognitive-Behavioral Procedure*, 4th ed., edited by Philip C. Kendall, 190–233. New York, NY: Guilford Press.

Stark, Kevin, William Streusand, Lauren S. Krumholz, and Puja Patel. 2010. "Cognitive-Behavioral Therapy for Depression: The ACTION Treatment Program for Girls." In *Evidence-Based Psychotherapies for Children and Adolescents*, 2nd ed., edited by John R. Weisz, and Alan E. Kazdin, 93–109. New York, NY: Guilford Press.

Stark, Kevin D., Mary G. Yancy, Sarah Schnoebelen, Jennifer Hargrave, and Johanna Molnar. 2011. *'ACTION' Workbook for Parents of Depressed Boys*. Ardmore, PA: Workbook Publishing.

Starr, Lisa R., and Joanne Davila. 2009. "Clarifying Co-Rumination: Associations with Internalizing Symptoms and Romantic Involvement among Adolescent Girls." *Journal of Adolescence* 32 (1): 19–37. doi:10.1016/j.adolescence.2007.12.005.

Stevens, Elizabeth A., and Mitchell J. Prinstein. 2005. "Peer Contagion of Depressogenic Attributional Styles Among Adolescents: A Longitudinal Study." *Journal of Abnormal Child Psychology* 33 (1): 25–37.

Stice, Eric, Katherine Presnell, and Sarah Kate Bearman. 2001. "Relation of Early Menarche to Depression, eating Disorders, Substance Abuse, and Comorbid Psychopathology among Adolescent Girls." *Developmental Psychology* 37 (5): 608–19.

Stone, Lindsey B., Benjamin L. Hankin, Brandon E. Gibb, and John R. Z. Abela. 2011. "Co-Rumination Predicts the Onset of Depressive Disorders during Adolescence." *Journal of Abnormal Psychology* 120 (3): 752–57. doi:10.1037/a0023384.

Stringaris, Argyris, Barbara Maughan, William S. Copeland, E. Jane Costello, and Adrian Angold. 2013. "Irritable Mood as a Symptom of Depression in Youth: Prevalence, Developmental, and Clinical Correlates in the Great Smoky Mountains Study." *Journal of the American Academy of Child and Adolescent Psychiatry* 52 (8): 831–40. doi:10.1016/j.jaac.2013.05.017.

Sullivan, Patrick F., Mechael C. Neale, and Kenneth S. Kendler. 2000. "Genetic Epidemiology of Major Depression: Review and Meta-Analysis." *American Journal of Psychiatry* 157 (10): 1552–62. doi:10.1176/appi.ajp.157.10.1552.

Swann, William B. Jr., Richard M. Wenzlaff, Ddouglas S. Krull, and Brett W. Pelham. 1992. "Allure of Negative Feedback: Self-Verification Strivings among Depressed Persons." *Journal of Abnormal Psychology* 101 (2): 293–306. doi:10.1037/0021-843X.101.2.293.

Task Force on Promotion and Dissemination of Psychological Procedures. 1995. "Training in and Dissemination of Empirically Validated Psychological Treatments: Report and Recommendations." *Clinical Psychologist* 48: 3–23.

Teunissen, Hanneke A., Caroline B. Adelman, Mitchell J. Prinstein, Renske Spijkerman, Evelien A. P. Poelen, Rutger C. M. E. Engels, and Ron H. J. Scholte. 2011. "The Interaction Between Pubertal Timing and Peer Popularity for Boys and Girls: An Integration of Biological and Interpersonal Perspectives on Adolescent Depression." *Journal of Abnormal Child Psychology* 39 (3): 413–23. doi:10.1007/s10802-010-9467-1.

Thapar, Anita, Stephan Collishaw, Daniel S. Pine, and Ajay K. Thapar. 2012. "Depression in Adolescence." *The Lancet* 379 (9820): 1056–67. doi:10.1016/S0140-6736(11)60871-4.

Timmons, Katherine A., and Thomas E. Joiner. 2008. "Reassurance Seeking and Negative Feedback Seeking." In *Risk Factors for Depression*, edited by K. S. Dobson and D. J. Dozois, 429–46. San Diego, CA: Elsevier Academic Press. doi:10.1016/B978-0-08-045078-0.00019-8.

Treatment for Adolescents with Depression Study Team, John March, Susan Silva, John Curry, Karen Wells, John Fairbank, Barbara Burns, et al. 2009. "The Treatment for Adolescents With Depression Study (TADS): Outcomes over 1 Year of Naturalistic Follow-Up." *The American Journal of Psychiatry* 166 (10): 1141–49. doi:10.1176/appi.ajp.2009.08111620.

Turner, Jr., Jackson E., and David A. Cole. 1994. "Developmental Differences in Cognitive Diatheses for Child Depression." *Journal of Abnormal Child Psychology* 22 (1): 15.

Van Tuijl, Lonneke A., Peter J. De Jong, B. Esther Sportel, Eva De Hullu, and Maaike H. Nauta. 2014. "Implicit and Explicit Self-Esteem and Their Reciprocal Relationship with Symptoms of Depression and Social Anxiety: A Longitudinal Study in Adolescents." *Journal of Behavior Therapy and Experimental Psychiatry* 45 (1): 113–21. doi:10.1016/j.jbtep.2013.09.007.

Verboom, Charlotte E., Jelle J Sijtsema, Frank C. Verhulst, Brenda W. J. H. Penninx, and Johan Ormel. 2014. "Longitudinal Associations between Depressive Problems, Academic Performance, and Social Functioning in Adolescent Boys and Girls." *Developmental Psychology* 50 (1): 247–57. doi:10.1037/a0032547.

Vitiello, Benedetto. 2009. "Combined Cognitive-Behavioral Therapy and Pharmacotherapy for Adolescent Depression." *CNS Drugs* 23 (4): 271–80.

Vitiello, Benedetto, Graham Emslie, Gregory Clarke, Karen Dineen Wagner, Joan R. Asarnow, Martin B. Keller, Boris Birmaher, et al. 2011. "Long-Term Outcome of Adolescent Depression Initially Resistant to Selective Serotonin Reuptake Inhibitor Treatment: A Follow-up Study of the TORDIA Sample." *Journal of Clinical Psychiatry* 72 (3): 388–96. doi:10.4088/JCP.09m05885blu.

von Knorring, Anne-Liis, Gunilla Ingrid Olsson, Per Hove Thomsen, Ole Michael Lemming, and Agnes Hultén. 2006. "A Randomized, Double-blind,

Placebo-controlled Study of Citalopram in Adolescents with Major Depressive Disorder." *Journal of Clinical Psychopharmacology* 26 (3): 311–15.

Vulser, Hélène, Hervé Lemaitre, Eric Artiges, Ruben Miranda, Jani Penttilä, Maren Struve, Tahmine Fadai, et al. 2015. "Subthreshold Depression and Regional Brain Volumes in Young Community Adolescents." *Journal of the American Academy of Child and Adolescent Psychiatry* 54 (10): 832–40.

Wagner, Karen Dineen. 2005. "Pharmacotherapy for Major Depression in Children and Adolescents." *Progress in Neuro-Psychopharmacology & Biological Psychiatry* 29 (5): 819–26. doi:10.1016/j.pnpbp.2005.03.005.

Wagner, Karen Dineen, Jeffrey Jonas, Robert L. Findling, Daniel Ventura, and Khalil Saikali. 2006. "A Double-Blind, Randomized, Placebo-Controlled Trial of Escitalopram in the Treatment of Pediatric Depression." *Journal of the American Academy of Child and Adolescent Psychiatry* 45 (3): 280–88. doi: 10.1097/01.chi.0000192250.38400.9e.

Wagner, Karen Dineen, Adelaide S. Robb, Robert L. Findling, Jianqing Jin, Marcelo M. Gutierrez, and William E. Heydorn. 2004. "A Randomized, Placebo-controlled Trial of Citalopram for the Treatment of Major Depression in Children and Adolescents." *The American Journal of Psychiatry* 161 (6): 1079–83. doi:10.1176/appi.ajp.161.6.1079.

Weersing, V. Robin, and John R. Weisz. 2002. "Community Clinic Treatment of Depressed Youth: Benchmarking Usual Care Against CBT Clinical Trials." *Journal of Consulting and Clinical Psychology* 70 (2): 299–310. doi:10.1037/0022-006X.70.2.299.

Weiss, Bahr, Thomas Catron, Vicki Harris, and Tam M. Phung. 1999. "The Effectiveness of Traditional Child Psychotherapy." *Journal of Consulting and Clinical Psychology* 67: 82–94. doi:10.1037//0022-006X.68.6.1094.

Weiss, Lauren A., Lin Pan, Mark Abney, and Carole Ober. 2006. "The Sex-Specific Genetic Architecture of Quantitative Traits in Humans." *Nature Genetics* 38 (2): 218–22.

Weissman, Myrna M., and Gerald L. Klerman. 1992. "Depression: Current Understanding and Changing Trends." *Annual Review of Public Health* 13: 319–39. doi:10.1146/annurev.pu.13.050192.001535.

Weissman, Myrna M., Susan Wolk, Risë B. Goldstein, Donna Moreau, Philip Adams, Steven Greenwald, Claudia M. Klier, Neal D. Ryan, Ronald E. Dahl, and Priya Wickramaratne. 1999. "Depressed Adolescents Grown Up." *Journal of the American Medical Association* 281 (18): 1707–13. doi:10.1001/jama.281.18.1707.

Wesselhoeft, Rikke, Merete J. Sørensen, Einar R. Heiervang, and Niels Bilenberg. 2013. "Subthreshold Depression in Children and Adolescents: A Systematic Review." *Journal of Affective Disorders* 151: 7–22. doi:10.1016/j.jad.2013.06.010.

Whitaker, Robert. 2015. "Anatomy of an Epidemic: The History and Science of a Failed Paradigm of Care." *The Behavior Therapist 38* (7): 192–8.

Whittle, Sarah, Renee Lichter, Meg Dennison, Nandita Vijayakumar, Orli Schwartz, Michelle L Byrne, Julian G Simmons, et al. 2014. "Structural Brain Development and Depression Onset During Adolescence: A Prospective Longitudinal Study." 171: 564–71.

Widiger, Thomas A., and Lee A. Clark. 2000. "Toward DSM—V and the Classification of Psychopathology." *Psychological Bulletin* 126 (6): 946–63. doi:10.1037/0033-2909.126.6.946.

Wilens, Timothy E., Joseph Biederman, and Thomas J. Spencer. 2002. "Attention Deficit/Hyperactivity Disorder Across the Lifespan." *Annual Review of Medicine* 53: 113–31. doi:10.1146/annurev.med.53.082901.103945.

Zarrouf, Fahd Aziz, Steven Artz, James Griffith, Cristian Sirbu, and Martin Kommor. 2009. "Testosterone and Depression: Systematic Review and Meta-Analysis." *Journal of Psychiatric Practice* 15 (4): 289–305. doi:10.1097/01.pra.0000358315.88931.fc.

# Author Biographies

**Rebecca A. Schwartz-Mette** is a licensed psychologist and assistant professor of clinical psychology at the University of Maine. She earned a dual PhD in child clinical and developmental psychology from the University of Missouri. Her program of research is focused on the intersection of depression and peer relations in childhood and adolescence. Her work has been published in top child clinical and developmental psychology journals and has been funded by the National Institute of Mental Health. She has extensive clinical assessment and intervention experience with children, adolescents, and adults in community, educational, clinical, and forensic settings.

**Hannah R. Lawrence,** MA, is a graduate student in the developmental-clinical track of the doctoral program in clinical psychology at the University of Maine. Her research examines the role of cognition in the development of depression in childhood and adolescence. She has research, intervention, and assessment experience working with preschoolers through adults in a range of settings. Her role as a graduate student contributes a unique perspective in developing this practical guide for trainees and practitioners.

**Douglas W. Nangle** is professor and the director of the doctoral program in clinical psychology at the University of Maine. He is a licensed psychologist with more than 20 years of experience in clinical practice, supervision, teaching, and research. His research examines the relations between social interactions and adjustment, with a particular focus on internalizing distress. His work regularly appears in top journals, and his publications include four books, including a recently released volume on the treatment of child and adolescent internalizing disorders published by Guildford Press.

**Cynthia A. Erdley** is professor of developmental psychology at the University of Maine. For over 20 years, she has mentored students in the developmental-clinical track of the doctoral program in clinical psychology and has taught courses focused on child and adolescent development. Her research has investigated the ways in which children's and adolescents' peer experiences relate to their adjustment, including depression. She has also examined the role of social-cognitive processes in behavior and psychological adjustment. Her work has been published in leading child clinical and developmental psychology journals.

**Laura A. Andrews,** BA, is a graduate student in the developmental-clinical track of the clinical psychology doctoral program at the University of Maine. Her current research examines the association between social interactions in peer relationships, specifically social rejection, and internalizing symptoms, such as depression and anxiety. She also has clinical experience with child and adolescent populations with treatment-resistant depression, suicidal behavior, and eating disorders.

**Melissa S. Jankowski,** BA, is a graduate student in the developmental-clinical track of the clinical psychology doctoral program at the University of Maine. She has research experience with evidence-based treatments for childhood and adolescent depression, as well as clinical experience with diverse populations in a variety of settings. Her current program of research centers on adolescent peer relations and their association with depression, self-injury, and suicide.

# Index

# OTHER TITLES IN OUR CHILD CLINICAL PSYCHOLOGY "NUTS AND BOLTS" COLLECTION

Samuel T. Gontkovsky, *Editor*

- *Learning Disabilities* by Charles J. Golden and Lisa K. Lashley
- *Intellectual Disabilities* by Charles J. Golden and Lisa K. Lashley
- *A Guide for Statistics in the Behavioral Sciences* by Jeff Foster
- *Childhood Sleep Disorders* by Connie J. Schnoes
- *Childhood and Adolescent Obesity* by Lauren A Stutts
- *Elimination Disorders: Evidence-Based Treatment for Enuresis and Encopresis* by Thomas M. Reimers

Momentum Press offers over 30 collections including Aerospace, Biomedical, Civil, Environmental, Nanomaterials, Geotechnical, and many others. We are a leading book publisher in the field of engineering, mathematics, health, and applied sciences.

Momentum Press is actively seeking collection editors as well as authors. For more information about becoming an MP author or collection editor, please visit http://www.momentumpress.net/contact

## Announcing Digital Content Crafted by Librarians

*Concise e-books business students need for classroom and research*

Momentum Press offers digital content as authoritative treatments of advanced engineering topics by leaders in their field. Hosted on ebrary, MP provides practitioners, researchers, faculty, and students in engineering, science, and industry with innovative electronic content in sensors and controls engineering, advanced energy engineering, manufacturing, and materials science.

**Momentum Press offers library-friendly terms:**
- *perpetual access for a one-time fee*
- *no subscriptions or access fees required*
- *unlimited concurrent usage permitted*
- *downloadable PDFs provided*
- *free MARC records included*
- *free trials*

The **Momentum Press** digital library is very affordable, with no obligation to buy in future years.

For more information, please visit **www.momentumpress.net/library** or to set up a trial in the US, please contact **mpsales@globalepress.com**.